5508

Every Knee Shall Bow

BY Joan Winmill Brown
No Longer Alone
Wings of Joy
Every Knee Shall Bow

Every Knee Shall Bow

compiled and edited by

Joan Winmill Brown

Fleming H. Revell Company
Old Tappan, New Jersey

Library of Congress Cataloging in Publication Data

Mail entry under title:

Every knee shall bow.

    Includes index.
    1. Jesus Christ—Person and offices—Collected works.
I. Brown, Joan Winmill.
BT199.E9   232   78-11521
ISBN 0-8007-0941-1

For my sons Bill, Jr., and David . . .
whose lives, as they were growing up,
taught me over and over again
what childlike love and trust really is . . .
with whom, down through the years,
I have shared the beauty of Jesus;
before whom every knee shall one day bow.

Contents

PART II

Introduction

. . . At the name of Jesus every knee shall bow in heaven and on earth . . . .

See Philippians 2:10

The desire to compile *Every Knee Shall Bow* came to me one Sunday morning, while sitting in the congregation of the Hollywood Presbyterian Church. We had just finished singing "There's Something About That Name," Bill and Gloria Gaither's moving hymn. In the worshipfulness of those moments, a newness of the magnificence of Jesus Christ came over me. I recalled how many times the name of Jesus had been my comfort and had sustained me, since I had given my life to Him.

How could I best relate the beauty of Christ that I was feeling at that moment to a friend or loved one, so that he or she could also experience His great Love?

It was then that I thought how much I would love to gather together some of the best of the writings of Christians of our day and those who, down through the years, have been affected also by the reality of the Saviour. I thought of passages of Scripture that have brought the incredible beauty of His life into mine—and poetry and prose that have given new insights into His Love.

How many times I have tried to express to others what has happened in my life, through Jesus Christ. F. B. Meyer's great poem describing what the apostle Paul was trying to convey concerning his experience, sums up so eloquently these longings:

9

Oh, could I tell ye surely would believe it!
Oh, could I only say what I have seen!
How should I tell or how can ye receive it,
How, till He bringeth you where I have been!

We can never experience the incredible beauty of Christ in our lives until we come to the place where Paul came—divested completely of self; or love as John loved; or in humble adoration worship as Mary Magdalene worshiped Him and knew the healing of His forgiveness.

It is my hope that through these collected works of the famous and unknown believers in the Living Christ, the readers will be drawn to Him and experience the joy of His presence in their lives. To those who already know Him, may this book bring you even closer to our Lord and strengthen your faith. Compiling it has meant just that for me.

I would like to express my gratitude to all those who so willingly gave their permission to have their writings included. To those who have gone to be with our Lord, my thanks to Him for the inspiration that their works continue to give.

To my husband, Bill, for his constant encouragement and help; to Ann Curtiss and Betsey Scanlan of Fleming H. Revell Company, who worked so diligently and lovingly with me; and to Debbie Brink for typing the manuscript with such a joyful spirit—my heartfelt thanks.

—J. W. B.
JOAN WINMILL BROWN

Part I

JESUS—HIS LOVE
Our Way of Knowing God Cares
JESUS—HIS FORGIVENESS
Our Promise of a New Beginning
JESUS—HIS DAILY PRESENCE
Our Comfort and Joy

Jesus—His Love

Our Way of Knowing God Cares

The King of Love my Shepherd is,
Whose goodness faileth never;
I nothing lack if I am His
And He is mine forever.

H. W. BAKER

How wonderful to know you are loved. You can face all the trials, the disappointments, the rejections of others, if you know that you as a person are *loved*.

It is hard perhaps to realize that God, who created this vast universe, could possibly care for the individual. For me, it has always been necessary to imagine an immense family—the Father caring for each of His children, as an earthly father does. He does not love the family in a general way, he loves each individual in a very special way.

In Jesus' life, here on earth, there was always concern and love for the individual. We read in John 5:5 of "a certain man" who had been ill for thirty-eight years and had come to the Pool of Bethesda, at a time when an angel was supposed to "trouble" the waters. The people believed that whoever was lowered into the water first would be healed. Somehow this "certain man" had managed to get to the Pool, but he had no one to help him into the water. Perhaps he had had someone who had been willing to bring him there, but could not wait for the angel. This man had been ill so long, they were probably tired of trying to help him—he was very much alone.

What a pathetic sight it must have been as Jesus approached that day. Crowds of people—sick, blind, lame, and paralyzed—all waiting—hoping—that they would be healed. Into this assembly of desperate, heartweary, suffering people came Jesus and this lonely, seemingly forgotten man stood out to Him. He went

15

over and healed him instantly: the love and concern of Jesus Christ for some-one, who had no one.

The parable that Jesus told of the lost sheep again speaks of His love for each one of us. The shepherd leaves the ninety-nine sheep safe in the fold and goes out to find that lost one. Finding it, he lays the animal on his shoulders and comes back, rejoicing. It would have been easy to say, "I have ninety-nine others, I am too busy and too tired to bother finding this one," but the shepherd cares for each one of his sheep.

With Jesus' love in our lives, we can rise above the grudging spirit and love another as he or she should be loved. It is a love that has been through difficult places itself, a love that has known rejection, but now has been lifted up into the magnificence of the light of Christ's love.

When we have this love in us we can face today, tomorrow, the days ahead, knowing we are being shepherded by our Saviour, who loved us so much that He was willing to die for us. The Cross illustrates that God is all love for He sent His Son to die, taking our guilt upon Him—the sacrificial Lamb.

Even when Jesus faced the Cross, He prayed for *us*. These words of His as He speaks to the Father are the embodiment of His true, self-sacrificing love for you and me:

> *Father, forgive them; for they know not what they do.*
>
> Luke 23:34
>
> —*J. W. B.*

> [I pray] That they all may be one; as thou, Father, art in me, and I in thee, that they also may be one in us . . . that they may be one, even as we are one: I in them, and thou in me, that they be made perfect in one . . . and that the world may know that thou hast sent me, and hast loved them, as thou hast loved me.
>
> John 17:21–23

Never has anyone given up so much. It is claimed (by him as well as by us) that he renounced the joys of heaven for the sorrows of earth, exchanging an eternal immunity to the approach of sin for painful con-tact with evil in this world. He was born of a lowly Hebrew mother in a dirty stable in this insignificant village of Bethlehem. He became a ref-ugee baby in Egypt. He was brought up in the obscure hamlet of Nazareth, and toiled at a carpenter's bench to support his mother and the other children in their home. In due time he became an itinerant preacher, with few possessions, small comforts and no home. He made friends with simple fishermen and publicans. He touched lepers and allowed harlots to touch him. He gave himself away in a ministry of healing, helping, teaching and preaching.

He was misunderstood and misrepresented, and became the victim of men's prejudices and vested interests. He was despised and rejected by his own people, and deserted by his own friends. He gave his back to be flogged, his face to be spat upon, his head to be crowned with thorns, his hands and feet to be nailed to a common Roman gallows. And as the cruel spikes were driven home, he kept praying for his tormentors, "Father, forgive them; for they know not what they do."

Such a man is altogether beyond our reach. He succeeded just where we invariably fail. He had complete self-mastery. He never retaliated. He never grew resentful or irritable. He had such control of himself that, whatever men might think or say or do, he would deny himself and abandon himself to the will of God and the welfare of mankind. "I seek not my own will," he said, and "I do not seek my own glory." As Paul wrote, "For Christ did not please himself."

This utter disregard of self in the service of God and man is what the Bible calls love. There is no self-interest in love. The essence of love is self-sacrifice. The worst of men is adorned by an occasional flash of such nobility, but the life of Jesus irradiated it with a never-fading incandescent glow.

Jesus was sinless because he was selfless. Such selflessness is love. And God is love.

JOHN R. W. STOTT

> Fairest Lord Jesus,
> Ruler of all nature,
> O thou of God and man the Son!
> Thee will I cherish,
> Thee will I honor
> Thou, my soul's glory, joy, and crown.
> Seventeenth-century German hymn

Jesus created love by revealing the essential dignity and lovableness of men. It is easy to notice a man's shabby coat, his defects in grammar, his peculiar ways: Jesus went deeper, and showed that every soul was a potential son of a King. Of a scorned, renegade tax-gatherer He said, "He also is a son of Abraham" (Luke 19:9). A woman whom all good people ostracised He treated with a dignity and courtesy that might have been given to a queen (Luke 7:37). And when He said, "Take heed that ye despise not one of these little ones" (Matthew 18:10), He was thinking, not only of the children, but of all the weak, defenceless, sensitive things of life. It does most mightily inspire love towards your fellowmen when you can see, as Jesus saw, upon every face that passes you in the street something of the image of God.

Jesus created love by dying for men. Every day of His life the disciples saw their Master squandering His strength for the sick and the sinful, and when Calvary came they knew that it was for sheer love of them that He had died. Can you continue to be unloving to any man, even the most unlovable, when you remind yourself—"It was for that man Jesus died"?

JAMES S. STEWART

He loves each one of us, as if there were only one of us.

SAINT AUGUSTINE

Let us try, all of us, to come closer to that unity of spreading Christ's love wherever we go. Love and compassion; have deep compassion for the people. People are suffering much: mentally, physically, in every possible way. So you are the ones to bring that hope, that love, that kindness.

Do you want to do something beautiful for God? There is a person who needs you. This is your chance.

MOTHER TERESA

Don't ever let me get so busy, Lord, that I forget to hold out the right hand of fellowship—to those I know and love, and to those I ought to know and love.

DALE EVANS ROGERS

However distasteful a service may be, or however disagreeable the person to whom it must be rendered, God is back of it all, and loved that person well enough to give

His Son to die for him. Dr. Guthrie was walking along the streets of Edinburgh, when he overtook a little girl carrying a child much too heavy for her. In a very gentle way Dr. Guthrie said: "My child, the baby is too heavy for you, isn't he?" With a shining face she made quick response: "No, sir; he's my brother." It makes a difference that one for whom I must toil and wait, whose burden I must bear, was one for whom Jesus died, and thus is bound to me with the cord of divine love.

J. WILBUR CHAPMAN

A new commandment I give unto you, That ye love one another; as I have loved you, that ye also love one another.

John 13:34

There was once a young girl who lived in an orphanage, who was so unattractive and awkward, so dull in personality, and a troublemaker too that the superintendent and her staff just could not bear her. Because they knew that no one would ever want to adopt such an unfeminine little girl, they planned a way of getting rid of her. Day and night they watched her, encouraging her to make a mistake so that they would have a reason for recommending that she be sent to a reform school.

One day their chance came. Although the young people were forbidden to leave the grounds, a staff member saw her sneak out the front gate. She climbed a tree, crawled out on a limb, and tied a note to it with a piece of string. Then she climbed down and returned to the orphanage. The superintendent and a number of the staff ran to see what she had done. When the superintendent took the note and began to read it to herself, tears rolled down her hardened cheeks.

"What does it say?" demanded the others. She held it out for them to read.

"Whoever finds this note, I love you," it said.

God did a similar thing. He wrote a note on a tree outside the wall of Jerusalem at a place called Golgotha. In essence this is what He said, "Whoever finds My Son, you will know that I love you."

TOM SHIPP

i want to keep wrapping my arms around the world,
and loving them.
    where they hurt.
    in ways that count.
    as Jesus would do.
Jesus and people and me.
that's all.

ANN KIEMEL

Lord, make me an instrument of Your peace.
Where there is hatred, let me sow love;
Where there is injury, pardon;
Where there is doubt, faith;
Where there is despair, hope;
Where there is darkness, light;
And where there is sadness, joy.

O Divine Master, grant that I may not
So much seek to be consoled as to console;
To be understood as to understand;
To be loved as to love;
For it is in giving that we receive;
It is in pardoning that we are pardoned;
And it is in dying
That we are born to eternal life.

SAINT FRANCIS OF ASSISI

In a world of convenience relationships, where life is easy come and easy go, human personalities are shattered by the shallowness of it all. Our Lord has said that if we have his kind of love for one another, the whole world will know that we are his disciples because of the quality of that love.

At the Last Supper our Lord took a cup and said, ". . . Drink of it, all of you; for this is my blood of the covenant, which is poured out for many for the forgiveness of sins" (Matthew 26:27, 28 RSV).

He was fulfilling the first great covenant God made with mankind— that one day out of the seed of Abraham every nation on earth should be blessed. Thank God for that covenant!

And he was fulfilling a new covenant that God had promised through Jeremiah when he said, "And no longer shall each man teach his neighbor and each his brother, saying, 'Know the LORD,' for they shall all know me, from the least of them to the greatest, says the LORD; for I will forgive their iniquity, and I will remember their sin no more" (31:34 RSV). Thank God for *that* covenant! God loves us so much that he is a covenant-making God! He desires all of us to drink of the same cup—to be a covenant-making people.

"By this all men will know that you are my disciples, if you have love for one another" (John 13:35 RSV). I know of nothing that the world is more hungry for than covenant love. This is our chance! "The whole creation is on tiptoe to see the wonderful sight of the sons of God coming into their own" (Romans 8:19 PHILLIPS).

Thank God for his creative love!

LOUIS H. EVANS, JR.

It is possible to be so active in the service of Christ as to forget to love Him.

P. T. FORSYTH

Though Jesus often addressed Himself to large audiences which gathered round Him, it is impressive how interested He was in individual men and women. It is touching to see the very special attention He gave to any man or woman who showed the least inclination toward Him. And His enormous patience with such people warms our hearts and stirs our spirits. It endorses what we ourselves have found to be true of Him. He loves us with an everlasting love. He draws us with tender understanding if we respond to His overtures of affection. Ultimately the decision rests with us. He will not override our wills. He will not force Himself upon us. He calls. We either come or turn to go our own way.

W. PHILLIP KELLER
Rabboni

Walk in love, as Christ also hath loved us, and hath given himself for us an offering and a sacrifice to God for a sweet-smelling savour.

Ephesians 5:2

Love doesn't always win . . . Neither does it lose. Christ, by his example, tells us to forgive even those who have not admitted and confessed their wrongdoing . . . even when they are not yet aware that they have hurt or wounded . . . even when they do not know he said, "Father, forgive them, for they know not what they do."

Beyond forgetting and leaving the hurt behind us, we can do something to heal the wound. Sometimes this works, sometimes it doesn't . . . Success is not guaranteed. But, remember—even Jesus did not win them all . . . .

Try . . . take the risk . . . in the doing there is freedom!

COLLEEN TOWNSEND EVANS
Start Loving

May we and all who bear Thy name
By gentle love Thy Cross proclaim,
The gift of peace on earth secure,
And for Thy Truth the world endure.

AUTHOR UNKNOWN

Jesus, though tall and slim, was a man of unbending strength. His years at his father's carpenter's bench vigorously wielding the tools of his trade had toughened and strengthened the sinews and muscles of his limbs. But while he was iron strong, he seemed flexible and unhardened.

He seemed stubbornly dedicated to principles; yet he was pliable and tender.

Martha loved his bluntness of speech, the way he never wasted words, and his honest, truthful directness; yet she was touched beyond belief by the utmost kindness which framed all his conversations. He was obviously filled with authority; yet he was human, warm, and touchable. Martha always thought of him as the most whole and healthy man she had ever seen. It seemed to Martha that Jesus, teacher and rabbi, was a most complete man.

When he was in her home, Martha found herself unable to do enough for him. She was skilled in serving, treating, and even healing others; yet his presence in her house inspired her to unbelievable heights of giving and doing. Jesus' slightest gesture or look was met by Martha's immediate consideration, and off she would fly to fulfill his need. She could not put her finger on the exact reason for her desire to serve him, only that it was so. It was as if he had touched a responsive chord deep within her being, and serving him became her most compelling urge.

Whenever word reached her that Jesus was teaching in Jerusalem, she went into a flurry of frenzied activity, for she knew he would come for a visit. It was such a short walk from the temple courtyard in Jerusalem to her front gate that Jesus rarely spent his evening meal or night's lodging any place but in Martha's spacious house. It was an unspoken agreement between them, and it was these visits which deepened the loving friendship between Martha, Mary, Lazarus, and Jesus.

With Jesus' visits, Mary grew pensive and quiet, "It is as if," she told Martha one night as they climbed the steps to the roof-top, "I want to store everything in my heart. I dare not miss a thing he says or does. I have the feeling I will someday wish I had listened more."

JOYCE LANDORF

> To those who fall, how kind Thou art;
> How good to those who seek;
> But what to those who find? Ah, this
> Nor tongue no pen can show:
> The love of Jesus, what it is,
> None but His loved ones know.
>
> BERNARD OF CLAIRVAUX

Dear Friend . . .

I just had to send a note to tell you how much I love you and care about you. I saw you yesterday as you were walking with your friends. I waited all day hoping you would want to talk with me also. As evening drew near, I gave you a sunset to close your day and a cool breeze to rest you. And I waited. But you never came. It hurt me, but I still love you because I am your friend.

I saw you fall asleep last night and I longed to touch your brow. So, I spilled moonlight on your pillow and your face. Again I waited, wanting to rush down so that we could talk. I have so many gifts for you. But you awakened late that next day and rushed off to work. My tears were in the rain.

Today you looked so sad, so all alone. It made my heart ache because I understand. My friends let me down and hurt me so many times, too. But I love you. Oh, if you would only listen to me. I really love you. I try to tell you in the blue sky and in the quiet green grass. I whisper it in the leaves on the trees and breathe it in the colors of the love songs to sing. I clothe you with warm sunshine and perfume the air with nature's scents. My love for you is deeper than the oceans and bigger than the biggest want or need in your heart.

If you only knew how much I want to help you. I want you to meet my Father. He wants to help you, too. My Father is that way, you know. Just call me, ask me, talk with me. I have so much to share with you. But, I won't hassle you. I'll wait because I love you.

Your friend,

JESUS

The Savior is waiting to enter your heart,
   Why don't you let Him come in?
There's nothing in this world to keep you apart,
   What is your answer to Him?
Time after time He has waited before,
   And now He is waiting again
To see if you're willing to open the door:
   O how He wants to come in.

RALPH CARMICHAEL

Love Him, and keep Him for thy friend,
who, when all go away, will not forsake
thee, nor suffer thee to perish in the end.

THOMAS À KEMPIS

In the French Revolution, a young man was condemned to the guillotine, and shut up in one of the prisons. He was greatly loved by many, but there was one who loved him more than all put together. How know we this? It was his best earthly friend, his own father, and the love he bore the son was proven in this way: When the lists were called, the father, whose name was exactly the same as the son's, answered to the name, and the father rode in the gloomy tumbril out to the place of execution, and his head rolled beneath the axe instead of his son's, a victim to mighty love. See here an image of the love of Christ for sinners. "Greater love hath no man than this; that he laid down his life for his friends." But Jesus died for the ungodly! He is the friend of sinners. There is no friendship like Christ's.

CHARLES H. SPURGEON

Thanks be to Thee, my Lord Jesus Christ,
For all the benefits Thou hast given me,
For all the pains and insults Thou hast
    borne for me.
O most merciful Redeemer, Friend, and
    Brother,
May I know Thee more clearly,
May I love Thee more dearly,
May I follow Thee more nearly. *Amen.*

Twelfth-century prayer

I have found a great many kind friends but Jesus is the best. He understands me so well, and has such a way of putting up with my frailties, and has promised to do so much for me, when all other loved ones swim away from my vision, and I can no more laugh with them over their joys or cry with them over their sorrows. Oh! when a man has trouble, he needs friends. When a man loses property, he needs all those of his acquaintances who have lost property to come in with their sympathy. When bereavement comes to a household, it is a comfort to have others who have been bereaved come in and sympathize. God is a sympathetic friend. O the tenderness of divine friendship.

THOMAS DE WITT TALMADGE

The older I grow in years, the more the
wonder and the joy increase when I see the
power of these words of Jesus—"I have
called you friends"—to move the human

heart. That one word "friend" breaks down
each barrier of reserve, and we have boldness in his presence. Our hearts go out in
love to meet his love.

CHARLES F. ANDREWS

He knows, He loves, He cares.
Nothing this truth can dim.
He gives the very best to those
Who leave the choice with Him.

AUTHOR UNKNOWN

George Matheson, shortly after he had become engaged to be married,
found out that he was going blind. When he told his fiancée she said, "I
cannot marry a blind man." Desperate, he thought of suicide, feeling
there was now no reason to live; but the love of Jesus Christ was stronger
than his desperation and through Matheson's experience we have been
given the moving hymn "O Love That Wilt Not Let Me Go."

O Love that wilt not let me go,
    I rest my weary soul in Thee;
I give Thee back the life I owe,
That in Thine ocean depths its flow
    May richer, fuller be.

O Light that followest all my way,
    I yield my flickering torch to Thee;
My heart restores its borrowed ray,
That in Thy sunshine's blaze its day
    May brighter, fairer be.

O Joy that seekest me through pain,
    I cannot close my heart to Thee;
I trace the rainbow through the rain,
And feel the promise is not vain
    That morn shall tearless be.

O Cross that liftest up my head,
    I dare not ask to fly from Thee;
I lay in dust life's glory dead,
And from the ground there blossoms red
    Life that shall endless be.

O Hope that lightenest all my way,
   I cannot choose but cleave to Thee;
And wrestle till the break of day,
Disclose the wisdom of the way
   In blessings yet to be.

                GEORGE MATHESON

In the weary,
waiting,
silence
of the night,
speak to me, Lord!
The others do—
haunting,
accusing,
forboding;
the body tosses
and
the heart grows tight,
and
sleep, elusive, fades into
the
weary,
waiting,
silence
of the night.

He speaks:
the mind,
preoccupied with sleeplessness,
is deaf.
Silently
He wraps me in His love;
so loved,
I rest.

          RUTH BELL GRAHAM
          Sitting by My Laughing Fire

When I am emotionally embittered or discouraged, when I experience that dull ache of loneliness, or I am saddened in the trough of some criticism or failure, he comes to comfort me. It is as though his healing power is extended to my neurotic feelings. If he can make a leper clean, he can make a neurotic normal. Often I ask Jesus to raise the hand which calmed the winds and waves of Gennesareth over my turbulent soul. Make me calm and tranquil, too. However, I firmly believe that God comes not only to comfort the afflicted, but also to afflict the comfortable.

There are times when he comes not to trouble me, but only to re-arrange my values or make me aware of someone in need; and always to challenge me to grow. I have never asked him for a problemless life or a plastic tranquility. I ask only for that peace which knows what is impor-tant and what is unimportant, only for that serenity which knows that I have been loved and that I am called to love.

JOHN POWELL

I praise Thee while my days go on;
I love Thee while my days go on:
Through dark and dearth, through fire
    and frost,
With emptied arms and treasure lost,
I thank Thee while my days go on.
ELIZABETH BARRETT BROWNING

We are loved! He took the first risk. We can dare to love, too. Nothing can threaten our sense of value. Nothing can undermine our confidence. Nothing can take God's love away. We can be real. We can help others become real, too: ". . . once you are Real you can't be ugly, except to people who don't understand."

There were times when giving and loving brought pain,
And I promised I would never let it happen again!
But I found out that loving was well worth the risk,
And that even in losing, you win.

I'm going to live the way He wants me to live.
I'm going to give until there's just no more to give.
I'm going to love, love 'til there's just no more love—
I could never, never outlove the Lord!

He showed us that only through dying we live.
And He gave 'til it seemed there was no more to give.
He loved when loving brought heartache and loss.
He forgave from an old rugged Cross.

I'm ~~~ to live.
I'~ ~~~ to give.
~ ~~~ love—
~~~ D!

GAITHER

~~~ ould take the malefactor's
~~~ ould ring through all history,
~~~ heroic pity; and well deserved
~~~ nnets of admiration which would
~~~ Jesus did this, and infinitely more
~~~ nalefactors but enemies to His own
~~~ der of wonders! But it meets with small
~~~ d us have heard of it, and treated it as of
little ~~~ as a pious legend; as a venerable fable; as an
unpracti~ ~~~ ose who know, believe, and admire, are cold
in their emo~ ~~~ regard to the story of the atonement. Herein is
love which oug~ ~o set our hearts on fire, and yet we scarcely maintain a smoldering spark of enthusiasm. Lord Jesus, be more real to
our apprehensions, and more completely the master of our affec-
tions.

CHARLES H. SPURGEON

CONSTRAINED BY LOVE

The love of Christ constraineth us; because we thus judge, that if one died for all,
then were all dead: And that he died for all,
that they which live should not henceforth
live unto themselves, but unto him which
died for them, and rose again.

2 Corinthians 5:14, 15

Be all my heart, be all my days,
Devoted to Thy single praise;
And let my glad obedience prove
How much I owe, how much I love.

ABRAHAM LINCOLN
Devotional

If you knew that there was One greater than yourself, who knows you better than you know yourself, and loves you better than you can love yourself; One who gathered into himself all great and good things and causes, blending in his beauty all the enduring color of life, who could turn your dreams into visions, and make real the things you hoped were true; and if that One had done one unmistakable thing to prove, even at the price of blood—his own blood—that you could come to him, would you not fall at his feet with the treasure of your years, your powers, your love? And is there not One such?

A. E. WHITHAM

There met in Jesus Christ all things that
can make man lovely and loveable.

GERALD MANLEY HOPKINS

O how He loves you and me.
O how He loves you and me;
He gave His life, what more could He give:
O how He loves you, O, how He loves me,
O how He loves you and me.

KURT KAISER

When the love of Christ comes into a
human life it is the greatest uplifting and
ennobling power of which the world has
any knowledge. It brings new birth, for it
brings Christ himself. For it no sacrifice is
too great, no piece of service too humble.

HOWARD W. GUINNESS

Most of us have never with our eyes seen Jesus near nor with our ears heard his voice, but we have, in some moment of hushed splendor, felt the brush of his garments. We have sensed the warmth of his love in our hearts. We have known hours of quiet inspiration when he bent low. We have been touched by the warmth of his presence. In our hearts we have heard the muted music of his voice.

Does he live?

Ask your own heart. For multitudes the answer is there.

GLENN ALTY CRAFTS

Were the whole realm of nature mine,
That were an offering far too small;
Love so amazing, so divine,
Demands my soul, my life, my all.

ISAAC WATTS

I do understand enough about myself to know that when I get to heaven, I'll be overjoyed just to stand in line, knowing at last I'm in His presence. His love does this to us. Love that is always giving. Oh, I just love Him. I love Him. How I long for you children to love Him too.

I have loved Jesus Christ all my life, but I think I had to surrender myself to Him before I knew how to love other people. In spite of all my success and all the happiness I tried to give my audiences, there was no personal happiness in me. I was a high-strung person by nature, but, thank heaven, I'm under the control of my Saviour now. I had no real happiness then. I have it now with Jesus.

ETHEL WATERS

. . . O Saul, it shall be
A Face like my face that receives thee; a Man like to me,
Thou shalt love and be loved by, forever: a Hand like this hand
Shall throw open the gates of new life to thee! See the Christ stand!

ROBERT BROWNING
Saul

How have we come to Christ today? Have we come like the Pharisees, to argue and demand a sign? Have we been aware of all the signs God has given already? Elizabeth Barrett Browning was right,

Earth's crammed with heaven,
And every common bush afire with God;
But only he who sees takes off his shoes;
The rest sit round it and pluck blackberries.

What more can Jesus do to convince us? Nothing. It is done. The Cross is the sign of his love. If we take him at his word and trust him with our lives, the power of his love will transform us and make us a sign to our generation that Christ is alive, of what life was meant to be, and what can happen to a person who trusts him completely.

LLOYD J. OGILVIE
Life Without Limits

Take my life and let it be
Consecrated, Lord, to Thee;
Take my moments and my days,
Let them flow in endless praise;
Take my hands and let them move
At the impulse of Thy love;
Take my feet and let them be
Swift and beautiful for Thee.

FRANCES RIDLEY HAVERGAL

Your love, dear Lord Jesus, overwhelms me. How can I begin to thank You, for You know the unloveliness of my life. But the knowledge of the depth of this Eternal Love helps me to begin each day— renewed—for You care about even the minutest detail of my life. In the turmoil and in the calm, Your love is unchanging, my Lord and my God. Amen.

—J. W. B.

guard would roll back the stone and allow me to anoint the body.

To my amazement, the stone had already been rolled aside! Inside the tomb the grave clothes lay—all in place—but the body of Jesus was gone. Alarmed, I ran back to the city—to the house where the disciples had spent the Sabbath. Awakening Peter and John, I told them someone had taken the body of the Lord.

I couldn't keep pace with them as they ran through the early light of dawn to the cemetery. By the time I had reached the tomb, my strength was gone, my grief uncontrollable.

Looking about for Peter and John, I suddenly became aware of an unearthly glow coming from the sepulcher. Stooping down I looked inside, and to my astonishment saw two figures in white, one sitting at the head of the grave clothes, the other at the feet of the place where Jesus' body had lain.

One of them, seeing my tears, asked, "Why are you crying?"

I said, "Because they've taken away my Lord and I don't know where they've put him."

I turned from the dazzling brightness of the angelic beings, sensing another's presence behind me. It was the gardener—or so I supposed.

"O Sir, if you have carried him away, please tell me where you've put him and I will take him away."

The figure spoke a single word. My heart leaped within me.

"Mary, " he said. And suddenly my grief and loneliness vanished.

"Master," I cried, and flung myself at his feet, clinging desperately to that body so ravaged on the tree.

"No," he said, gently disengaging me. "Do not hold me now. I have not yet gone up to the Father. Go and tell the disciples that I am going up to my Father and your Father, to my God and your God."

I watched him go, through blinding tears of joy—then marveled at how quickly I returned to the Upper Room to tell the others that I had seen the Lord—that he had risen as he said.

It was not until much later that I learned something I shall always remember—and treasure: That morning he rose from the dead, the Lord appeared *first* to the least worthy of all his followers. A woman who once walked the streets—possessed of devils—she was the *first* to hear the resurrection news. And to her was given the privilege of telling all the others.

Such love—such compassion—such forgiveness.

Do you wonder that I—*that woman*—Mary of Magdala in Galilee—call him *Master?*

                                                                    DICK ROSS

Jesus—His Forgiveness

Our Promise of a New Beginning

The Bible says that when you bring your sins to Him, He will blot them out like a cloud. Did you see that cloud this morning? It is gone. It will never come again. It has absolutely disappeared forever.

CORRIE TEN BOOM

People all over the world are weighed down with the guilt of their pasts. Psychiatrists' couches are busier than ever with people trying to rid themselves of guilt. Jesus promises His love and forgiveness to all who will come to Him, realizing their need and their failings. "If we confess our sins, he is faithful and just to forgive us our sins, and to cleanse us from all unrighteousness" (1 John 1:9).

Only Jesus can see the unseen you. We cannot hide from the intensity of His gaze; we cannot pretend any more when we come into His presence. The acts of hypocrisy which have become almost unconscious to us as we relate to other people, seem tawdry compared to His example. His perfect life strips away the facade and leaves us naked and ashamed. But the peace of His forgiveness brings an inner joy and quietness of heart, for He loves and forgives us unconditionally. People often love us for what they see on the outside—Jesus loves *in spite* of what He sees on the inside.

Billy Graham recalls that the night he came to Christ he did not have any tears. But when he went home, he looked out of the window at the North Carolina sky and cried over his sins and said, "Oh, God, forgive me." Then the most wonderful peace swept over him. "From that moment on, I've known my sins were forgiven." The more we love Christ, the more we realize the depths from which He has brought us.

"Father, forgive them; for they know not what they do." These were the first words that Jesus spoke from the Cross. His executioners must have been astounded to hear this Man, whose hands were being brutally nailed to a wooden beam, cry out these words. These men were hammering spikes into the very hands of the One who had been sent by God to forgive them. He had preached "Love your enemies"—now in excruciating agony His love and concern for others was still uppermost in His mind. He had known the hatred, condemnation, indifference of His enemies, but still He asked God to forgive them.

This same Jesus comes into our lives and waits to forgive us. When we are completely honest before Him an incredible miracle happens. We are cleansed of all our mistakes and are given a new beginning. We may still remember the past, but God has promised:

> As far as the east is from the west, so far hath
> he removed our transgressions from us.
>
> Psalms 103:12
>
> —J. W. B.

Jesus had the ability to understand all people, no matter what their position in society. On one occasion He was dining with a prominent religious leader named Simon. While they were eating, a repentant prostitute came into the hall where the meal was being served and began to wash the feet of Jesus with her tears and dry them with her hair. The religious leader was shocked and began to look at Jesus with doubt. He thought, "If this man were a prophet He would know who and what sort of person this woman is who is touching Him . . . ."

Jesus, sensing his thoughts, told him this story: "A certain moneylender had two debtors; one owed five hundred denarii [a denarius was then a day's wage], and the other fifty. When they were unable to repay, he graciously forgave them both. Which of them therefore will love him more?"

Simon must have wondered, what's the purpose of this story? He probably shrugged as he answered, "I suppose the one to whom he forgave more."

Jesus told him that was the right answer. Then He reminded Simon that when He had come into his house as a guest, Simon had ignored all the normal courtesies of the day. "You gave Me no water for My feet, but she has wet My feet with tears, and wiped them with her hair. You gave Me no kiss; but she, since the time I came in, has not ceased to kiss My feet."

Then Jesus turned to the woman and reassured her that her sins h been forgiven.

The other guests at the dinner party were astounded. They ask "Who is this man who even forgives sins?" (Luke 7:49).

We know that Jesus often dined with the social elite but defende social outcasts.

BILLY GRAHAM
How to Be Born

I never knew repentance until I learned
from the wounds of Jesus.

MARTIN LUTHER

MARY OF MAGDALA

We watched him die—Salome, Mary and I—who had fo Master from Galilee to care for his daily needs as the end dre the day he was crucified we could do no more than stand a aloof from the hostile crowd that pressed closely about the t

An awesome darkness covered the city. The elements see our grief.

About three o'clock in the afternoon a stillness settled o Those who had come to mock and jeer now stood uneasil waiting.

Suddenly the silence was broken by a loud voice from center cross:

"Father, into thy hands I commit my spirit!"

And the head—marred more than any man's—dropp breast. It was finished.

When the crowd had dispersed, a man from Arima of Joseph claimed the body, having received permissi authorities. We followed the little procession down t cemetery and watched as they prepared the body fo it tenderly in a new tomb carved in rock, in which laid. Then a great stone was rolled across the entr

How can I tell you of the long day that follow from the household, yet pacing the floor many t journey," I tried to stamp out the dreadful crosses—and the tragic form of that One, rejecte

When the Sabbath had finally passed—very took spices and returned to the garden with t

> Nothing in this low and ruined world
> bears the meek impress of the Son of God
> so surely as forgiveness.
>
> ALICE CARY

What is it that binds you and keeps you from being a free man or a free woman? What memories of the past, what relationships of the present, what uncertainties of the future keep you bound?

What cycle of condemnation are you locked into? What inflexibility, what habit patterns keep you incarcerated in the prison of life? Why is it that you react in certain situations the way you do and find it so difficult to grow to be the liberated, unique person you were meant to be?

The living Christ moves among us, and our bound and imprisoned spirits are suddenly lifted. He takes hold of us, lifts us up. Tenderly we see him face to face!

Suddenly we are experiencing communion with him. In his presence, the prison garb no longer fits. It binds. It distresses. In such a moment, we want more than anything else to be a free person.

Paul said, "Now the Lord is the Spirit, and where the Spirit of the Lord is, there is freedom" (2 Corinthians 3:17 RSV).

It is the Spirit who comes within us as we reach out for these symbols of costly grace. And as we eat of the bread and drink of the cup, he comes to live in us, and from within us he does a magnificent thing.

From deep below the level of words, he assures us that in spite of it all, we are forgiven. That whatever distracts us and gives us a sense of guilt or uncertainty when we come into his presence can be washed away. And he reminds us that he can take the raw material of our future and shape it into something significant and splendid.

LLOYD JOHN OGILVIE
The Cup of Wonder

REMEMBERED SIN

I made a lash of my remembered sins.
I wove it firm and strong, with cruel tip,
And though my quivering flesh shrank from the scourge,
With steady arm I plied the ruthless whip.

For surely I, who had betrayed my Lord,
Must needs endure this sting of memory.
But though my stripes grew sore, there came no peace,
And so I looked again to Calvary.

His tender eyes beneath the crown of thorns
Met mine; His sweet voice said, "My child, although
Those oft-remembered sins of thine have been
Like crimson, scarlet, they are now like snow.

"My blood, shed here, has washed them all away,
And there remaineth not the least dark spot,
Nor any memory of them; and so
Should you remember sins which God forgot?"

I stood there trembling, bathed in light, though scarce
My tired heart dared to hope. His voice went on:
"Look at thy feet, My child." I looked, and lo,
The whip of my remembered sins was gone!

MARTHA SNELL NICHOLSON

MUTUAL FORBEARANCE

Forbearing one another, and forgiving
one another, if any man have a quarrel
against any: even as Christ forgave you, so
also do ye.

Colossians 3:13

May we each with each agree,
Through Thy uniting grace:
Our gift shall Thine accepted be,
Our life be love and praise.

ABRAHAM LINCOLN
Devotional

THE WOMAN TAKEN IN ADULTERY

. . . He that is without sin among
you, let him first cast a stone at her.

John 8:7

Why didn't Jesus condemn an adulteress? Does it mean that He condones this sin or any other sin? No person who ever comes to know the
pure, sinless Christ would say that He condones our sins. He hated sin
as He hated hell. Sin is against Him and everything He stood for. Sin
was the one thing He warred against. It was sin that crucified Him.

There are two reasons why He didn't condemn the woman. First, it

wasn't necessary. Others had already condemned her. Her own con-
science had condemned her. The law of Moses, which is the law of God,
had condemned her. The one who transgresses God's way is condemned
—let us make no mistake about that.

Second, Jesus had something far better to offer than condemnation.
"For God sent not his Son into the world to condemn the world; but that
the world through him might be saved" (John 3:17). Instead of condemnation, He gave her forgiveness. I say gave—she didn't earn it. She
couldn't earn it. How could she turn back the pages of her life and wipe
away the stains? What had been done had been done.

And let us be slow to become self-righteous in the presence of this
fallen woman. Not only are there sins of the body—there are sins of the
heart, sins of the mind, sins of the disposition. We are all sinners. We
have all come short of His glory. Under the power of His presence, this
woman had come to hate her sin and to want to live above it.

CHARLES L. ALLEN

         . . . marla is married to a man
   who loves marla in spite of her past.
      he trusts her and believes in her and forgives
         her just as Jesus has . . . .

ANN KIEMEL

   We call Jesus the Christ, and he in us, and we in him,
   Live in perfect harmony in Eden the land of life,
   Giving, receiving, and forgiving each other's trespasses.

ROBERT BROWNING

Every day Peter was hearing Jesus speak with a strange, incredible
authority he had never heard in any voice before. Every day he was
watching Jesus at work, and observing with growing admiration and
wonder how more than equal He was to all emergencies. Every day he
was seeing Jesus in contact with shattered, futile lives, and these lives
going back to the world again changed in a way in which he had always
thought it was absolutely impossible for anyone but God to change
them. There was more even than that. In his own heart Peter knew that
none but God could forgive sin: yet in his own heart there was a voice
telling him with utter certainty that this Jesus had forgiven him, and had
indeed done more than that, for He was not breaking the power of sin in
His servant's life—a work which only the God of heaven could do. That

is how Peter found who Christ was. When all is said, how else can anyone find it? This Jesus does for me what only God can do. This Jesus floods my being as only the Father of heaven could flood it. What can I do but confess it? This is divine! "Thou art the Christ, the Son of the living God."

JAMES S. STEWART

THE LOOK

The Saviour looked on Peter. Ay, no word,
No gesture of reproach: the heavens serene,
Though heavy with armed justice, did not lean
Their thunders that way: the forsaken Lord
Looked only on the traitor. None record
What the look was, none guess; for those who have seen
Wronged lovers loving through a death-pang keen,
Or pale-cheeked martyrs smiling to a sword,
Have missed Jehovah at the judgment-call.
And Peter, from the height of blasphemy,—
"I never knew this man"—did quail and fall,
As knowing straight *that* God—and turned free
And went out speechless from the face of all,
And filled the silence, weeping bitterly.

THE MEANING OF THE LOOK

I think that look of Christ might seem to say,
"Thou Peter! art thou then a common stone
Which I at last must break my heart upon,
For all God's charge to his high angels may
Guard my foot better? Did I yesterday
Wash *thy* feet, my beloved, that they should run
Quick to deny me 'neath the morning sun?
And do thy kisses, like the rest, betray?
The cock crows coldly.—Go, and manifest
A late contrition, but no bootless fear!
For, when thy final need is dreariest,
Thou shalt not be denied, as I am here:
My voice to God and angels shall attest,
"Because I know this man, let him be clear."

ELIZABETH BARRETT BROWNING

Here is Christian identity: I know my past, where I came from. I came from God. I know what went wrong. I tried to play God instead of being satisfied to be a real man. I know my future. My destiny is Christ. And I know the present. I can face myself now—my problems, my hang-ups, my assets, my faults—because I have turned myself over to God.

LEIGHTON FORD

The day that I stopped running, this God found me.
Empty, trembling,
shaken with guilt and shame I came.
In a way I cannot draw with words
   he loved me
     forgave me
      restored
       and gave me his own Name.
Say what you will,
but he met me then,
put in my heart
a homesickness for heaven.
I have heard the still, small Voice
and called him Friend.
      and I believe in God.

WILLIAM ALFRED PRATNEY

The dying Jesus is the evidence of God's anger toward sin; but the living Jesus is the proof of God's love and forgiveness.

LORENZ EIFERT

THE UNFAILING FRIEND

What a friend we have in Jesus,
  All our sins and griefs to bear!
What a privilege to carry
  Everything to God in prayer!
O what peace we often forfeit,
  O what needless pain we bear,
All because we do not carry
  Everything to God in prayer.

JOSEPH SCRIVEN

The Lord Jesus said it first. He said it to the two disciples of John who heard that He was the Lamb of God. They knew very little about Him, but they followed Him. Perhaps they would not even have ventured to speak, but "Jesus turned, and saw them following," and spoke to them. Then they asked Him where He dwelt, and He said, "Come and see!" Philip said it next. He had found Christ himself, and at once he told his friend Nathanael about it, "Come and see!" Is it not said still? Oh, "Come and see!" Look into the Saviour's glorious and loving face, and see what a lovely and precious Saviour He is! Come and see how ready He is to receive you, and to bless you. Come and see what He has done for you; see how He loved you and gave Himself for you; how He lived and suffered and bled and died for you! Come and see what gifts He has for you—forgiveness and peace, His Spirit and His grace, His joy and His love!

                                                          FRANCES RIDLEY HAVERGAL

What Christ did had to be done, or we should never have had forgiveness; we should never have known God. But he, by taking on himself our responsibilities and by dying our death, has so revealed God to us as to put forgiveness within our reach.

                                              JAMES DENNEY

Unto him that is able to keep you from falling, and to present you faultless before the presence of his glory with exceeding joy.

                                              Jude 24

A story that has been handed down from Victorian England tells of a soldier who had been punished many times for major offenses. Now he was in the guardhouse again.

Before he was to enter the Colonel's office, a sergeant asked if he could speak for the soldier. "Sir, I know that flogging, solitary confinement, disgrace—everything has been tried to change this man. May I take the liberty of suggesting one other thing?"

"What is that?" asked the officer.

"Sir, he has never been forgiven."

"Forgiven!" exclaimed the officer. But he thought for a few moments and then requested the offending soldier be brought in. Instead of ordering his punishment the Colonel looked at the soldier and said, "We forgive you."

The effect of this was that the soldier, who had shown nothing but contempt and was thought to be completely incorrigible, broke down and wept. The years went on to prove that his life was changed and this act of kindness gave the Queen's regiment a soldier of the finest caliber. The story was told by one who for years had him under close scrutiny.

> Therefore if any man be in Christ, he is a
> new creature: old things are passed away;
> behold, all things are become new.
> 2 Corinthians 5:17

Like a blind man I wandered
So lost and alone—
Like a beggar—so helpless—
Without God or His Son.
Then the Savior in mercy
Heard and answered my cry—
And, oh, what a difference
Since Jesus passed by.

All my yesterdays are buried
In the deepest of the sea;
That old load of guilt I carried
Is all gone! Praise God, I'm free!
Looking for a bright tomorrow
Where no tears will dim the eye—
Oh! There's such a difference
Since Jesus passed by!

Since Jesus passed by,
Since Jesus passed by.
Oh! What a difference,

Since Jesus passed by!
Well, I can't explain it,
And I cannot tell you why,
But, Oh! What a difference—
Since Jesus passed by.

WILLIAM J. GAITHER

God's ways are not man's ways. Nor are His thoughts our thoughts. His Son would not grow up sheltered from the rough and tumble of His times. He would not be walled around with soft, sanctimonious surrounds. He would not be nurtured within the safe seclusion of a spiritual ivory tower. He would not be the product of some exclusive religious school like the Sanhedrin.

God's Son—God in man—would grow up fully exposed to the abrasive stresses and strains of His day. He would mature as a man amongst men. He would be One who had tasted and drunk deeply from the stream of human struggle, labor, and sweat, just to survive.

This is one of the great glories of our God. He is not a remote being detached from our desperate earth days. He is not a sublime deity who never entered the turmoil of our earth struggle. He is God, very God, who took on Himself the form of a man. He lived amongst us most of His earthly life as a carpenter's child who became a skilled craftsman in His own right. Our life was His life. Our delights were His delights. Our sorrows were His sorrows.

This makes Him so approachable. This endears Him to us. This draws us to Him with the quiet reassurance that He knows, He understands, He identifies with us in all our difficulties.

W. PHILLIP KELLER
Rabboni

One day John Ruskin, the nineteenth-century writer, was walking in the streets of London and became fascinated with the mud left by a recent rainstorm. He began to wonder just what inorganic elements composed the substance and decided to have a sample analyzed. The report came back: sand, clay, soot, and water.

As he thought about the findings, it occurred to him that these were the very same elements from which jewels and gems are formed. From sand comes the agate, onyx, carnelian, jasper, and amethyst; from clay comes the ruby, emerald, topaz, and sapphire; and from soot the diamond. The London mud had the same elements as precious jewels!

Man cannot change the mud into priceless stones—only the Creator —and only He can change our lives from the seemingly worthless persons that we are into those who have been transformed by the love and forgiveness of Jesus Christ.

> I went very unwillingly to a society in Aldersgate Street, where one was reading Luther's preface to the Epistle to the Romans. While he was describing the change which God makes in the heart through faith in Christ, I felt my heart strangely warmed. I felt I did trust in Christ, Christ alone for salvation; and an assurance was given me that He had taken away my sins, even mine, and saved me from the law of sin and death.
>
> JOHN WESLEY

One evening I invited Him into my heart. What an entrance He made! It was not a spectacular, emotional thing, but very real. Something happened at the very center of my life. He came into the darkness of my heart and turned on the light. He built a fire on the hearth and banished the chill. He started music where there had been stillness, and He filled the emptiness with His own loving, wonderful fellowship. I have never regretted opening the door to Christ and I never will—not into eternity!

ROBERT BOYD MUNGER

James Boswell, Jr., said, "No one ever really forgives another—except he bears the penalty of the other's sin against him." Jesus on the cross is the perfect example of that kind of substitution. God loves us that much!

You say you feel unworthy? Join the crowd!

You long, with all your heart, to be a better person? Remember—God accepts you . . . right now . . . exactly as you are. And if you accept him as he is, the miracle will happen. You and he—together—will be able to do something about what you would like to be!

COLLEEN TOWNSEND EVANS
Start Loving

Jesus, today i've been anxious for EVERYTHING.
this is sin.
i confess it.
take the intensity of my life
   and channel it into smooth-flowing gestures
   and uncomplicated, paced hours.

ANN KIEMEL

A CHILD'S EVENING PRAYER

Jesus, tender Shepherd, hear me;
   Bless Thy little lamb to-night;
Through the darkness be Thou near me,
   Keep me safe till morning light.

All this day Thy hand has led me,
   And I thank Thee for Thy care;
Thou hast clothed and warmed and fed me;
   Listen to my evening prayer.

Let my sins be all forgiven!
   Bless the friends I love so well!
Take me, when I die, to Heaven,
   Happy, there with Thee to dwell.

MARY L. DUNCAN

   And when they came to the place which
is called The Skull, there they crucified
him, and the criminals, one on the right
and one on the left. And Jesus said,
"Father, forgive them; for they know not
what they do."

Luke 23:33, 34 RSV

   Agape love, unconditional love, affirming love—there it was, nailed to
the cross and praying a prayer of forgiveness! The world can never
understand that love until it experiences that love, because that love is
not native to mankind. Human love has its limits. Go beyond them, and
our love is all over: "We are friends to the bitter end, but this is the bitter
end." Not so with Christ. He loved us to the end.

LOUIS H. EVANS, JR.

Lord Jesus Christ, thank You for loving me and taking this shattered life into Your tender, understanding hands. Thank You for forgiving and forgetting the past with all of its failures—the sins that kept me from walking each day with You. Teach me, by Your Holy Spirit, to live so closely to You that my life may be used to help pick up the pieces of other people's lives, so that they too may know Your forgiveness, my Lord and Saviour. Amen.

—J. W. B.

Jesus—His Daily Presence

Our Comfort and Joy

Jesus cares about our being comforted in the land of the living, in this period of history before He comes back and before we die. But we are not only to be comforted by the Holy Spirit who dwells in us. We are to have His help so that we can comfort each other.

EDITH SCHAEFFER

One of the greatest problems facing the world today is loneliness—the feeling that we are *completely* alone. It happens, this overwhelming emotion, sometimes in solitude and even in a crowd. There is no one, it seems, who can understand the heartache and frustration that faces us each day.

The presence of Jesus Christ in our lives is the most beautiful thing that can happen to us, for then we are never alone again! The lonely widow sitting in her room; the businessman, called upon to make important decisions; the mother, with all her responsibilities, as she raises her children; the young person, perilously walking through today's world; each one of us, in whatever circumstance we find ourselves, can know our Lord's presence and experience each day His joy and comfort.

When Jesus told His disciples of His imminent departure how they must have grieved and panicked. To think they would no longer be able to rely on Him each day to guide them. No more would they know the warmth and compassion of His friendship and love. So often this happens in our own lives when someone we care for deeply either has to leave us for a long time or—the ultimate sorrow—dies.

But Jesus promised that the disciples would not be alone. God would send a Comforter. He said, "I will not leave you comfortless: I will come to you" (John 14:18).

I once visited a woman in a very poor neighborhood, whose room was filled with such joy. She had been ill for years, but her face was radiant as she spoke of the comfort that Jesus Christ gave her each minute, of every hour, of every day. "I know I am not alone," she said. "Jesus is with me and His love and comfort are all I need." She was suffering greatly, but she could see beyond all the suffering to the day when she would not only feel His presence, she would be able to see Him, face-to-face.

We can all know this Comforter, the Holy Spirit, in our lives. When we give ourselves completely to Jesus, His presence comes to be with us and we never have to face another day without His divine guidance and strength.

> . . . *God hath sent forth the Spirit of his Son*
> *into your hearts . . . .*
>
> Galatians 4:6
>
> —*J. W. B.*

I take life a day at a time.
I ask Him for guidance and strength just for
   that day.
I do not have yesterday, nor tomorrow—just
   today.
When I accept that day for what is in it, I will
   find miracles in it.
Jesus tells me, "Take therefore no thought
   [don't worry overmuch] for the morrow . . .
   Sufficient unto the day is the evil thereof"
   (Matthew 6:34). That has saved me oceans
   of anxiety.
In other words, I have enough to handle, with
   God's help, on this one day. I am content to
   leave the rest in His hand, content that He
   will not leave me *comfortless.*
I thank God for the little things and the big
   things in every day: for life itself, for a world
   of beauty to live in, and for the beauty that
   outweighs the evil; for sunset and sunrise
   and another day to work for Him; for the love
   others have for me, and the love I have to
   share with them; for the gift of laughter; for

the talents He has put in my hands; for His
Presence all along the road.
I talk with Him and I walk with Him.
I pray without ceasing, audibly when I am alone,
silently in the presence of others.
I seek His pardon immediately when I have gone
out of line in thought, word, or deed, when
I do those things I know I ought not to do
and when I am not doing the things I know I
should be doing.
I remind myself constantly of His promise, "Lo,
I am with you *always*."

DALE EVANS ROGERS
Where He Leads

Speak to Him, thou, for He hears, and Spirit with
Spirit can meet—
Closer is He than breathing, and nearer than hands
and feet.

ALFRED TENNYSON

How easy for me to live with You, O Lord!
How easy for me to believe in You!
When my mind parts in bewilderment or falters,
when the most intelligent people see no further
than this day's end
and do not know what must be done tomorrow,
You grant me the serene certitude
that You exist and that You will take care
that not all the paths of good be closed,
Atop the ridge of earthly fame,
I look back in wonder at the path
which I alone could never have found,
a wondrous path through despair to this point
from which I, too, could transmit to mankind
a reflection of Your rays.
And as much as I must still reflect
You will give me.
But as much as I cannot take up
You will have already assigned to others.

ALEKSANDR SOLZHENITSYN

> O Lord my God, in thee do I put my
> trust: save me from all them that persecute
> me, and deliver me: Lest he tear my soul
> like a lion, rending it in pieces . . . .
>
> Psalms 7:1, 2

My friends told me that God was real . . . but I already knew that. They said there is a God-sized vacuum in each of us, and until it is filled with God we will never have true peace . . . I was beginning to know that. But then they told me something I had never known—they told me how to find God!

They said I wouldn't find Him by doing good or by working harder.

They said I wouldn't find Him through any efforts of my own.

They said I would find Him through a Person . . . through a Person so much like myself that He would understand my needs, yet Someone so thoroughly *God* that He could feed my hungry spirit.

At last I understood. At last I had been shown the Way. My friends urged me to follow it . . . to give Jesus my impoverished life and let Him make something useful out of it. And so I did. It was quiet . . . and simple . . . and very, very real. I said yes to Jesus Christ . . . and the God I had known to be real—but far away—came into my life.

What a difference there is between a vague sort of faith and a personal relationship with a living Christ! He has given me direction and a goal—and nothing has ever been quite the same for me. If I had to describe in a few words how my life has been changed by becoming a Christian, I would borrow these words from Jesus: "The man who wants to save his life will lose it; but the man who loses his life for my sake will find it" (Matthew 16:25 PHILLIPS).

Left to ourselves, we find this world a lonely place. No matter how many friends we have, or how big the family, we feel cut off from a warmth and love we can't describe . . . . It's always "out there somewhere"—until we open our hearts and let the Holy Spirit "in here." He is a part of God Himself, and He will keep us company as long as we live on this earth.

COLLEEN TOWNSEND EVANS
A New Joy

COMFORTED BY THE SPIRIT

When the Comforter is come, whom I
will send unto you from the Father, even
the Spirit of truth, which proceedeth from
the Father, he shall testify of me.

John 15:26

In the hour of my distress,
When temptations me oppress,
And when I my sins confess—
Sweet Spirit, comfort me.

ABRAHAM LINCOLN
Devotional

Come, Holy Spirit, I need Thee!
Come, Sweet Spirit, I pray!
Come, in Thy strength and Thy power;
Come in Thy own gentle way.

Come, like a spring in the desert,
Come, to the withered of soul;
O let Thy sweet, healing power
Touch me and make me whole.

Come, as a wisdom to children,
Come, as new sight to the blind,
Come, Lord, as strength to my weakness;
Take me: soul, body, and mind.

Come, as a rest to the weary,
Come, as a balm for the sore;
Come, as a dew to my dryness,
Fill me with joy evermore.

WILLIAM J. AND GLORIA GAITHER

What is it that hits me, that hits us all when a scream arises within us and fear takes over and we cry out in a silent cry that no one hears but God, "I can't. It is impossible. What am I doing? What have I gotten into!"? If we have asked the Lord for His will, and He really has shown us, then what we have started to do is a double thing of looking at the waves, the unchanging circumstances, and then taking a measure of credit for what we already have been doing, rather than dwelling on the wonder of the fact that He has been doing it for us or through us. There has to be a sustaining trust, a continuing trust, a moment-by-moment trust in the Lord in whom we have put our faith when we have asked Him to call us, to tell us to *come*. If the Lord has said, "Come—do this, do that," we have to remember that, of course, it will be impossible to us, but we must continue to believe that *He* is able. The trust must be an active, unfaltering reality—or we will also begin to sink, because there is no promise that the circumstances will always change.

> . . . Blessed are all they that put their trust
> in him.
>
>   Psalms 2:12
>
>   EDITH SCHAEFFER

> Are you looking unto Jesus now, in the
> immediate matter that is pressing, and re-
> ceiving from him peace? If so, he will be a
> gracious benediction of peace in and
> through you.
>
> OSWALD CHAMBERS

A missionary friend told me of a time of great crisis in her life. They were stationed in a primitive area, and her husband had to go on an extended trip into "the bush." He had scarcely left when one of the children contracted polio. Soon the others developed a minor malady with alarmingly similar symptoms. My friend felt desperate. How could she bear the responsibilities—day and night nursing, the anxiety at home as well as concern for her husband who was venturing into unknown territory?

Eventually the episode had a happy ending. The children recovered; the mother lived through a very difficult time; and the father returned safely, rejoicing because of souls who came to know Christ because he had gone to them with the Gospel message.

Our conversation had started because she was comforting me during a period in which my tribulations loomed large. But as she talked they seemed small compared to some of her experiences.

"How did you survive?" I asked her. "Of course I know you must have prayed and prayed and prayed!"

"Actually, I didn't," she confessed. "I was too exhausted to formulate the words. I moved like an automaton from one task to the next one. God understood, and I felt His presence. Also, He gave me a simple sentence that kept me going day and night. I want to share it with you. Try it; it will sustain you through anything: I've proven its worth. I just affirmed: 'For this, I have Jesus.' "

WINOLA WELLS WIRT

I can do all things through Christ which strengtheneth me.

Philippians 4:13

IN HIM CONFIDING

Sometimes a light surprises
   The Christian while he sings;
It is the Lord who rises
   With healing in his wings.
When comforts are declining
   He grants the soul again
A season of clear shining,
   To cheer it after rain.

WILLIAM COWPER

Know that Our Lord is called in Scripture the Prince of Peace, and hence, wherever He is absolute Master, He preserves peace.

SAINT FRANCIS DE SALES

Peace I leave with you, my peace I give unto you: not as the world giveth, give I unto you. Let not your heart be troubled, neither let it be afraid.

John 14:27

The storm was raging. The sea was beating against the rocks in huge, dashing waves. The lightning was flashing, the thunder was roaring, the wind was blowing; but the little bird was sound asleep in the crevice of the rock, its head tucked serenely under its wing. That is peace: to be able to sleep in the storm!

In Christ we are relaxed and at peace in the midst of the confusions, bewilderments and perplexities of this life. The storm rages, but our hearts are at rest. We have found peace—at last!

BILLY GRAHAM
Peace With God

The road to the Mount of Ascension invariably passes through the shadowed Garden of Gethsemane, and over the steep ascent of Calvary, and then down into the Garden of the Grave. "We must through much tribulation enter into the kingdom of God." But amidst it all it is possible to be kept in unbroken peace, like that which possessed the heart of Jesus, enabling Him calmly to work a miracle of healing amid the tumult of His arrest.

His peace *passeth all understanding* (Philippians 4:7). It cannot be put into words. It defies analysis. It must be felt to be understood. The thing most like it is the gladsomeness of a child in its father's home, where wealth and love and wise nurture combine to supply all its need; but even that falls short of the glorious reality. "Eye hath not seen, nor ear heard, neither have entered into the heart of man, the things which God hath prepared for them that love him. But God hath revealed them unto us by his Spirit . . . we have the mind of Christ" (1 Corinthians 2:9, 10, 16).

F. B. MEYER

The peace of Jesus Christ is not the peace of the conqueror, it is the peace of the loser in this life. The heroes of Rome found that their garlands wilted quickly and their victories ended in bitterness. Not so our Lord! Jesus Christ became a victim that He might become the eternal Victor. Thus when we sign God's peace conditions in His Name we have lost, we have surrendered command of our lives; but because of the vicarious sacrifice of Christ we receive the Holy Spirit of God who raises the dead. Out of the fellowship of Christ's sufferings comes the power of the Resurrection. Not by the might of the legions, not by the power of the atom, but *by my Spirit,* says the Lord.

SHERWOOD E. WIRT
The Cross on the Mountain

Tell Him about the heartache,
And tell Him the longings, too.
Tell Him the baffled purpose
When we scarce know what to do.

Then leaving all our weakness
With the One divinely strong,
Forget that we bore a burden
And carry away a song.

PHILLIPS BROOKS

CHRIST'S POWER IN DIFFICULTY

If we follow this precept and if we regard this event not as an effect of chance, not as a fatal necessity of nature, but as a result indispensable, inevitable, just and holy, of a decree of His providence, conceived from all eternity to be executed at such an hour and in such a manner, we shall adore in humble silence the impenetrable loftiness of His secrets; we shall venerate the sanctities of His decrees, we shall bless the acts of providence and submit our will to that of God Himself. We shall wish with Him and for Him the thing He has willed in us and for us from all eternity.

BLAISE PASCAL

Lord, what a change within us one short hour
    Spent in Thy presence will prevail to make!
    What heavy burdens from our bosoms take,
    What parched grounds refresh as with a shower!
We kneel, and all around us seems to lower;
    We rise, and all, the distant and the near,
    Stands forth in sunny outline brave and clear;
We kneel, how weak! we rise, how full of power!
Why, therefore, should we do ourselves this wrong,
Or others, that we are not always strong,
    That we are ever overborne with care,
    That we should ever weak or heartless be,
Anxious or troubled, when with us is prayer,
    And joy and strength and courage are with Thee!

RICHARD C. TRENCH

The ground of our hope is Christ in the world, but the evidence of our hope is Christ in the heart.

MATTHEW HENRY

Hitherto have ye asked nothing in my name: ask, and ye shall receive, that your joy may be full.

John 16:24

Christ attributes all He does and says to the Father, and this makes God's name no longer terrible to us, but comforting.

MARTIN LUTHER

Christ claims our help in many a strange disguise;
Now, fever-ridden, on a bed He lies;
Homeless He wanders now beneath the stars;
Now counts the number of His prison bars;
Now bends beside us, crowned with hoary hairs.
No need have we to climb the heavenly stairs,
And press our kisses on His feet and hands;
In every man that suffers, He, the Man of Sorrows, stands!

AUTHOR UNKNOWN

Tragedy hits all of us in different degrees throughout our lives. When it hit Joni Eareckson her whole world was shattered. A beautiful young life, suddenly paralyzed by a diving accident—her future condemned to a wheelchair. Jesus Christ took her tragedy and turned it into a triumph. Joni's example of faith and trust in her Saviour has spoken to so many thousands of people. In her book *Joni* she describes her battle as she lay completely helpless in the hospital:

My studies in the Scriptures began in earnest now, along with other Christian literature. Writings by Francis Schaeffer and C. S. Lewis seemed like a breath of fresh air compared with Marx, Hesse, and the non-Christian books I'd read. I began to sense a direct application of and appreciation for the Word of God in my life. For the first time, I saw meaning for me in the Bible. My own "fiery trials" were now a little easier to cope with as I saw how I fit in with God's scheme of things, especially through reading the Psalms. "The Lord will sustain him [me] upon his [my] sickbed . . ." (Psalms 41:3 New American Standard).

Pressures seemed greatest at night. Perhaps therapy had gone badly that day. Or no one came to visit . . . Whatever the problem, I'd want to cry. I felt even more frustrated because I couldn't cry, for there was no one to wipe my eyes and help me blow my nose. The Scriptures were encouraging, and I'd apply the reality and truth of them to my own special needs. During these difficult midnight hours, I'd visualize Jesus standing beside my Stryker. I imagined Him as a strong, comforting person with a deep, reassuring voice, saying specifically to me, "Lo, I am with you always. If I loved you enough to die for you, don't you think I ought to know best how to run your life even if it means your being paralyzed?" The reality of this Scripture was that He was with me, now. Beside me in my own room! That was the comfort I needed.

I discovered that the Lord Jesus Christ could indeed empathize with my situation. On the cross for those agonizing, horrible hours, waiting for death, He was immobilized, helpless, paralyzed.

Jesus did know what it was like not to be able to move—not to be able to scratch your nose, shift your weight, wipe your eyes. *He was paralyzed on the cross.* He could not move His arms or legs. Christ knew exactly how I felt! "Therefore, since we have a great high priest who has gone into heaven, Jesus the Son of God, let us hold firmly to the faith we profess. For we do not have a high priest who is unable to sympathize with our weaknesses, but we have one who has been tempted in every way, just as we are . . ." (Hebrews 4:14, 15 New International Version).

Before my accident, I didn't "need" Christ. Now I needed Him desperately. When I had been on my feet, it never seemed important that He be part of my decision-making—what party to go to, whether to go to a friend's house or a football game, etc. It didn't seem that He would even be interested in such insignificant things. But, now that my life was reduced to the basic life-routines, He was a part of it because He cared for me. He was, in fact, my only dependable reality.

> I lay my "whys"
> before Your Cross
> in worship kneeling,
> my mind too numb
> for thought,
> my heart beyond
> all feeling.
>
> And worshiping,
> realize that I
> in knowing You
> don't need a "why."
>
> RUTH BELL GRAHAM
> *Sitting by My Laughing Fire*

The LORD is my shepherd; I shall not want. He maketh me to lie down in green pastures: he leadeth me beside the still waters. He restoreth my soul: he leadeth me in

the paths of righteousness for his name's
sake. Yea, though I walk through the valley
of the shadow of death, I will fear no evil:
for thou art with me . . . .

Psalms 23:1–4

When Dr. J. Wilbur Chapman was traveling through the Scottish high-
lands, he met a little shepherd boy tending his sheep. "Do you know the
Twenty-third Psalm?" he asked the boy. He did not, and so Dr. Chapman gave him the first five words—The Lord is my shepherd—and told
him to have a word for each finger of his hand. Months later Dr. Chapman traveled through the same section and decided to visit the boy. Not
finding him, he inquired at a near-by hut, where he found the lad's
mother. She told him the story of how her boy had perished in a fearful
blizzard during the winter. He had always treasured the five words of
the Psalm and he was specially impressed by the fourth word *my*. He
would frequently say the words and, holding onto his fourth finger,
would repeat: "My Shepherd, My Shepherd." "When his body was
found in the deep snow," said his mother, "his two hands were seen
projecting from the snow. He was clasping his fourth finger—and we
knew what that meant." Perhaps there are many who repeat the opening
words of this Psalm who cannot say from the heart: "Jesus is my
Shepherd."

KEITH L. BROOKS

Turn your eyes upon Jesus,
Look full in His wonderful face,
And the things of earth will grow strangely dim
In the light of His glory and grace.

HELEN H. LEMMEL

At all times we would be wise to walk a little closer to Christ. This is
one sure place of safety. It was always the distant sheep, the roamers, the
wanderers, which were picked off by the predators in an unsuspecting
moment. Generally the attackers are gone before the shepherd is alerted
by their cry for help. Some sheep, of course, are utterly dumb with fear
under attack; they will not even give a plaintive bleat before their blood
is spilled.

The same is true of Christians. Many of us get into deep difficulty beyond ourselves; we are stricken dumb with apprehension, unable even to call or cry out for help; we just crumple under our adversary's attack.

But Christ is too concerned about us to allow this to happen. Our Shepherd wants to forestall such a calamity. He wants our summer sojourn to be in peace. Our Lord wants our mountaintop times to be tranquil interludes. And they will be if we just have the common sense to stay near Him where He can protect us. Read His Word each day. Spend some time talking to Him. We should give Him opportunity to converse with us by His Spirit as we contemplate His life and work for us as our Shepherd.

W. PHILLIP KELLER
A Shepherd Looks at Psalm 23

He giveth more grace when the burdens grow greater,
He sendeth more strength when the labors increase;
To added affliction He addeth His mercy,
To multiplied trials, His multiplied peace.

When we have exhausted our store of endurance,
When our strength has failed ere the day is half done,
When we reach the end of our hoarded resources,
Our Father's full giving is only begun.

His love has no limit, His grace has no measure,
His power no boundary known unto men;
For out of His infinite riches in Jesus
He giveth and giveth and giveth again.

ANNIE JOHNSON FLINT

He said to me, "My grace is sufficient for you, for my power is made perfect in weakness." I will all the more gladly boast of my weaknesses, that the power of Christ may rest upon me. For the sake of Christ, then, I am content with weaknesses . . . for when I am weak, then I am strong.

2 Corinthians 12:9, 10 RSV

Christ can triumph in a weaker man than
I am, if there be any such.

SAMUEL RUTHERFORD

Dr. S. D. Gordon tells of an old Christian woman whose age began to tell on her memory. She had once known much of the Bible by heart. Eventually only one precious bit stayed with her, "I know whom I have believed, and am persuaded that He is able to keep that which I have committed unto Him against that day." By and by part of that slipped its hold, and she would quietly repeat, "That which I have committed unto Him." At last as she hovered on the borderland between this and the spirit world, her loved ones noticed her lips moving. They bent down to see if she needed anything. She was repeating over and over again to herself the one word of the text, "Him—Him—Him." She had lost the whole Bible but one word. But she had the whole Bible in that one word.

AUTHOR UNKNOWN

What though my joys and comforts die?
    The Lord my Saviour liveth;
What though the darkness gather round?
    Songs in the night He giveth;
No storm can shake my inmost calm,
    While to that refuge clinging;
Since Christ is Lord of heaven and earth,
    How can I keep from singing?

ROBERT LOWRY

Though our Saviour's Passion is over,
His compassion is not.

WILLIAM PENN

The world hopes for the best but Jesus
Christ offers the best hope.

JOHN WESLEY WHITE

Lord, Thou hast suffered, Thou dost know
The thrust of pain, the piercing dart,
How wearily the wind can blow
Upon the tired heart.

He whom Thou lovest, Lord, is ill.
O come, Thou mighty Vanquisher
Of wind and wave, say, Peace, be still,
Eternal Comforter.

AMY CARMICHAEL

The Christian should never forget that he has a Friend who stands by him, a Friend who knows all about fear because He "set His face to go to Jerusalem," aware that the cross and death were waiting for Him there. The faith that this Risen Christ is beside him and that He is quite capable of controlling the future whatever evil may come, is a source of serenity and courage to many a humble Christian believer.

GORDON POWELL

COMFORT

Speak low to me, my Saviour, low and sweet
From out the hallelujahs, sweet and low,
Lest I should fear and fall, and miss Thee so,
Who art not missed by any that entreat.
Speak to me as to Mary at Thy feet!
And if no precious gums my hands bestow,
Let my tears drop like amber, while I go
In reach of Thy divinest voice complete
In humanest affection—thus, in sooth,
To lose the sense of losing. As a child,
Whose song-bird seeks the wood for evermore,
Is sung to in its stead by mother's mouth,
Till, sinking on her breast, love-reconciled,
He sleeps the faster that he wept before.

ELIZABETH BARRETT BROWNING

The reason why Christ chose the hard
way of the cross was, among other things,
that he saw beyond it.

S. J. REID

Think you to escape
What mortal man can never be without?
What saint upon earth has ever lived apart from cross and
    care?
Why, even Jesus Christ, our Lord, was not even for one
    hour free from His passion's pain.
Christ says, "He needs must suffer,
Rising from the dead,
And enter thus upon his glory."
And how do *you* ask for another road
Than this—the Royal Pathway of the Holy Cross?

THOMAS À KEMPIS

Now I saw in my dream that the highway up which Christian was to
go was fenced on either side with a wall, and that wall was called Salvation. Up this way, therefore, did burdened Christian run, but not without great difficulty, because of the load on his back. He ran thus till he
came to a place somewhat ascending; and upon that place stood a Cross,
and a little below, in the bottom, a sepulcher. So I saw in my dream that
just as Christian came up to the Cross, his burden loosed from off his
shoulders and fell from his back and began to tumble, and so continued
till it came to the mouth of the sepulcher, where it fell in, and I saw it no
more.

JOHN BUNYAN
Pilgrim's Progress

Christ be with me, Christ before me, Christ behind me,
Christ in me, Christ beneath me, Christ above me,
Christ on my right, Christ on my left,
Christ when I lie down, Christ when I sit down, Christ
    when I arise,
Christ in the heart of every man who thinks of me,
Christ in the mouth of every one who speaks of me,
Christ in every eye that sees me,
Christ in every ear that hears me.

SAINT PATRICK

I have a great need for Christ; I have a
great Christ for my need.

CHARLES H. SPURGEON

DESPISED AND REJECTED

(Because none has come to help him in his hour of distress the hero of the poem grows embittered toward all men:)

> This bitter night
> I will make fast my door
> That hallow friends may trouble me no more.

(But in the night a knock is heard, and a Voice pleads:)

> Rise, let me in . . .
> My Feet bleed, see My Face,
> See My Hands bleed that bring thee grace,
> My Heart doth bleed for thee,
> Open to Me.

(All night long the knocking continues—till at daybreak the wretched man hears the footsteps fade away, "echoing like a sigh." On opening the door he sees:)

> Each footprint marked in blood and on my door
> The mark of blood forevermore.

CHRISTINA G. ROSSETTI

Counsellors are warned not to get involved emotionally with their patients, lest this involvement hinder them from doing their best. But Jesus Christ always speaks the truth in love (Ephesians 4:15). In the Upper Room, he told Peter the truth about himself, and tried to guide Peter into the place of victory. Unfortunately, Peter rejected the truth, and even argued with it; the result was shameful failure. Some people hold back the truth because they think this is one way to show love. Others tell the truth but have no love. Jesus Christ is able to blend both truth and love, and this makes him an effective Counsellor.

As our Counsellor, Jesus encourages us. "Let not your heart be troubled!" Why wouldn't their hearts be troubled? He had just told them that Peter would deny him and that one of their number was a traitor! On top of this, he had told them that he was leaving them to go back to the Father. Their hearts were troubled, deeply so; and so he sought to encourage them and prepare them for the demands that lay before them. He told them about the Father's house. He told them about the Holy Spirit, the "Comforter," the "Encourager" (for that is what the word comfort really means). A good counsellor does not protect us from the problems of life; instead, he prepares us for life's problems and helps us face them honestly and courageously. "God is our refuge and strength, a very present help in trouble" (Psalm 46:1). As our refuge, he hides us; as our strength, he helps us. We do not leave our Counsellor merely with good advice; he sends us away with the strength we need to do what he tells us to do.

WARREN W. WIERSBE

"But we see Jesus . . . ."—Hebrews 2:9

I don't look back: God knows the fruitless efforts,
   The wasted hours, the sinning, the regrets;
I leave them all with Him who blots the record,
   And mercifully forgives, and then forgets.

I don't look forward, God sees all the future,
   The road that, short or long, will lead me home,
And He will face with me its every trial,
   And bear for me the burdens that may come.

I don't look round me; then would fears assail me,
   So wild the tumult of earth's restless seas;
So dark the world, so filled with woe and evil,
   So vain the hope of comfort or of ease.

I don't look in; for then am I most wretched;
   Myself has naught on which to stay my trust;
Nothing I see save failures and short-comings,
   And weak endeavors crumbling into dust.

But I look up—into the face of Jesus,
   For there my heart can rest, my fears are stilled;
And there is joy, and love, and light for darkness,
   And perfect peace, and every hope fulfilled.

ANNIE JOHNSON FLINT

Jesus, the very thought of Thee
   With sweetness fills my breast;
But sweeter far Thy face to see
   And in Thy presence rest.
Amen.
Latin twelfth century,
Translated by EDWARD CASWALL

Come unto me, all that . . . are heavy
laden, and I will give you rest.

Matthew 11:28

The life of faith is not a life of mounting
up with wings, but a life of walking and
not fainting . . . Faith never knows where
it is being led, but it loves and knows the
One who is leading.

OSWALD CHAMBERS

Your joy in the Lord is to be a far deeper thing than a mere emotion. It
is to be the joy of knowledge, of perception, of actual existence. It is a far
gladder thing to be a bird, with all the actual realities of flying, than only
to feel as if you were a bird, with no actual power of flying at all. Reality
is always the vital thing.

The lark soars singing from its nest,
    And tells aloud
His trust in God, and so is blest
    Let come what cloud.

He has no store, he sows no seed,
Yet sings aloud, and doth not heed.
Through cloudy day or scanty feed,
    He sings to shame
Men who forget in fear of need
    A Father's name.

The heart that trusts forever sings,
And feels as light as it has wings;
A well of peace within it springs.
    Come good or ill,
Whate'er to-day or morrow bring,
    It is His will.

HANNAH WHITALL SMITH

If Christ were here tonight, and saw me tired,
    And half afraid another step to take,
I think He'd know the thing my heart desired,
    And ease that heart of all its throbbing ache.

If Christ were here in this dull room of mine,
   That gathers up so many shadows dim,
I am quite sure its narrow space would shine,
   And kindle into glory around Him.

If Christ were here, I might not pray so long;
   My prayer would have such little way to go;
'Twould break into a burst of happy song,
   So would my joy and gladness overflow.

If Christ were here tonight, I'd touch the hem
   Of His fair, seamless robe, and stand complete
In wholeness and in whiteness; I, who stem
   Such waves of pain, to kneel at His dear feet.

If Christ were here tonight, I'd tell Him all
   The load I carry for the ones I love—
The blinded ones, who grope and faint and fall,
   Following false guides, nor seeking Christ above.

If Christ were here! Ah, faithless soul and weak,
   Is not the Master ever close to thee?
Deaf is thine ear, that canst not hear Him speak;
   Dim is thine eye, His face that cannot see.

Thy Christ is here, and never far away;
   He entered with thee when thou camest in;
His strength was thine through all the busy day;
   He knew thy need, He kept thee pure from sin.

Thy blessed Christ is in thy little room,
   Nay more, the Christ Himself is in thy heart;
Fear not, the dawn will scatter darkest gloom,
   And heaven will be of thy rich life a part.

                    MARGARET E. SANGSTER

To satisfy the burning thirst of tormented souls nothing will do but to take them to the well of living waters, to true fellowship with Christ.

                    PAUL TOURNIER

In one of the guiding verses of my life, Psalms 37:5, we are told, "Commit your way to the Lord, Trust also in Him, and He will do it" (New American Standard). The first seven verses of Psalm 37 give us clear direction and encouragement: Fret not because of evildoers; do not worry, or actually, stop worrying; don't be overly concerned because of evildoers; but delight in the Lord and He'll give you the desires of your heart.

Also, in Proverbs 3:5, 6 we are told, ". . . lean not unto thine own understanding. In all thy ways acknowledge him, and he shall direct thy paths." These verses of Scripture have been mainstays to me as I have trusted Him to guide me in the right direction.

I have learned that when I look at my circumstances, it is easy to become discouraged and defeated, for I am not making myself available to God. But Scripture tells us the solution: "Set your mind on the things above, not on the things that are on earth. For you have died and your life is hidden with Christ in God" (Colossians 3:2, 3 New American Standard). I realize from these verses that I am to look to Christ in every kind of situation—to set my sights and affection on Him, and then I will have victory.

VONETTE Z. BRIGHT

Christ does not leave us comfortless, but we have to be in dire need of comfort to know the truth of His promise.

It is in times of calamity . . .
    in days and nights of sorrow and trouble
        that the presence
            the sufficiency
                and the sympathy of God grow very sure
                and very wonderful.

Then we find out that the grace of God is sufficient
for all our needs
    for every problem
    and for every difficulty
for every broken heart, and for every human sorrow.

It is in times of bereavement that one begins to understand
the meaning of immortality.

PETER MARSHALL
"The Problem of Falling Rocks"

God sometimes passes us into the valley
of shadow that we may learn the way, and
know how to lead others through it into the
light. To get comfort, we must comfort with
the comfort wherewith we ourselves have
been comforted. In wiping the tears of
others our own will cease to fall.

F. B. MEYER

And He was only thirty-three . . .
The year had come to spring—
And He hung dead upon a tree,
Robbed of its blossoming.
Sorrow of sorrows that Youth should die
On a dead tree 'neath an April sky.
And He was only thirty-three . . .
Anthems of joy be sung—
For, always, the Risen Christ will be
A God divinely young.
Glory of glories, a Tree, stripped bare,
Shed now Faith's blossoms everywhere.

VIOLET ALLEYN STOREY

In a children's hospital, I stood with my hand in a mother's hand. Her
little girl had died. She looked like a little angel. On that little girl's dead
face there was such an expression of peace!

"Oh, what joy it must be for that little child to be with Jesus! She will
be so happy in heaven."

"I believe that, too," the mother said, "but Corrie, you don't know
how wounded I am. I loved my little girl so very much. Why did the
Lord take her away from me?"

"I do not know, but God knows. He understands you. He loves you
and He loves that little girl."

There are moments when the suffering is so deep that one can hardly
talk to a person. What a joy it is then to know that the Lord understands.
No pit is so deep that the Lord is not deeper still. Underneath us are the
everlasting arms—and the Lord understands.

CORRIE TEN BOOM
He Cares, He Comforts

He shall cover thee with his feathers, and
under his wings shalt thou trust: his truth
shall be thy shield and buckler.

Psalms 91:4

Those who live in the Lord never see
each other for the last time.

Old German motto

We picture death as coming to destroy; let us rather picture Christ as
coming to save. We think of death as ending; let us rather think of life as
beginning, and that more abundantly. We think of losing; let us think of
gaining. We think of parting; let us think of meeting. We think of going
away; let us think of arriving. And as the voice of death whispers, "You
must go from earth," let us hear the voice of Christ saying, "You are but
coming to Me!"

NORMAN MACLEOD

Christ has made of death a narrow, starlit
strip between the companionships of yesterday and the reunions of tomorrow.

WILLIAM JENNINGS BRYAN

Martha's heart was broken because of the death of her brother,
Lazarus. To her Jesus said, "Thy brother shall rise again," but that gave
her very little comfort. She said, "I know that he shall rise again in the
resurrection at the last day," but to her that was so far away. And the
final resurrection seems so strange and vague.

Then Jesus said to her the most beautiful and comforting word that
has ever been spoken in the presence of death: "I am the resurrection,
and the life: he that believeth in me, though he were dead, yet shall he
live: and whosoever liveth and believeth in me shall never die."

To comment on those words of our Lord is like trying to describe a
rainbow or a sunset. Human words are so inadequate. You can't describe in words the sound of a gentle breeze rustling through the trees
on a hot summer day, or the melody of a pipe organ, or the beauty of a
rose, or the depth of a mother's love. In those words Christ reveals the
glorious truth that it is possible for a human being to be forever beyond
the reach of death.

CHARLES L. ALLEN

Two things are important in Jesus' speaking of Himself being "the resurrection and the life," and then afterwards weeping real tears, with real anger and sorrow. First, it is not wrong to weep, and it is not wrong to be angry at death and at Satan who causes death. It is not wrong to long for the change—that will come after Jesus comes back—to come quickly to this abnormal world. Your weeping *in all that* is possible while Jesus is weeping with you. It is when you or I turn away with bitterness and anger *at* God, instead of joining in His weeping, that it becomes a separation and sinfulness, rather than a running into the Lord's arms.

EDITH SCHAEFFER

> He that comforts all that mourn
> Shall to joy your sorrow turn:
> Joy to know your sins forgiven,
> Joy to keep the way to heaven,
> Joy to win his welcome grace,
> Joy to see Him face-to-face.
>
> CHARLES WESLEY

We don't always understand why calamity comes to us, but we do know that our greatest tragedy can be turned into God's greatest opportunity. We know that we can literally lay every problem at the feet of Jesus and watch Him perform the miracles we need. We know we can sense His closeness and presence in our lives as we praise Him and thank Him in anticipation of the way He is going to work everything out according to our good and His glory (Romans 8:28).

God always keeps His promise!

PAT BOONE

My father used to say to us, when we were children and had to go away from home for a while, "Children, don't forget, when Jesus takes your hand, then He holds you tight. And when Jesus keeps you tight, He guides you through life. And when Jesus guides you through life, one day He brings you safely home."

CORRIE TEN BOOM
He Cares, He Comforts

> Jesus Christ is not a crutch; He is the
> ground to walk on.
>
> LEIGHTON FORD

It is a paradox that the Christ Who died upon the cross should be able to bring such comfort to those who fear suffering and death, yet so it is. Professor Arnold Toynbee, the greatest living authority on world history . . . concluded his magnum opus, ten large volumes on the history of mankind. In these books he traces the rise and fall of civilisation after civilisation. He analyses the reasons why they rose and fell, the outside pressure, the internal corruption. Naturally we ask, will our civilisation also crash to destruction? Toynbee's answer is "Not necessarily. It depends on the religious response we make to the dangerous situation in which we find ourselves." He then describes a dream he had years ago—a dream which obviously made a deep spiritual impression upon him at the time and which has been a source of comfort and inspiration ever since. In his dream he pictured himself in Ampleforth Abbey in Yorkshire. Above the altar is suspended from the ceiling a huge cross. In his dream Professor Toynbee saw himself clinging to the foot of the cross. He heard a voice saying, "Amplexus, expecta." (Cling and wait.) So Toynbee concludes his mighty study of history by giving this same message to mankind, afflicted as we are by all kinds of fears, "Cling to the cross and wait." The cross brings home to us the reality of the forgiving love of God and such "perfect love casteth out fear." Again the cross speaks to us of God's power to overcome—eventually—every kind of evil. In this faith let us learn the art of accepting the future.

GORDON POWELL

When we set out on this quest, we found ourselves moving in the midst of a mighty host, but, as we have pressed forward, the marchers, company by company, have fallen out of the race . . . And now, as we stand and gaze with our eyes upon the farther shore, a single figure rises from the flood and straightway fills the whole horizon. There is the Savior.

ARNOLD J. TOYNBEE
A Study of History

Your Holy Spirit enfolds me—making me realize I am not alone. Thank You for Your strength, Your wisdom and the comfort of Your presence. Even in the most agonizing times I have the knowledge that You are there, Lord. When all I can do is whisper Your name, it is enough. You hear. You care. You understand. My praise and adoration, Lord Jesus. Amen.

—*J. W. B.*

Part II

JESUS—HIS BIRTH
   Our Pre-announced Gift From God
JESUS—HIS LIFE AND MINISTRY
   Our Divine Example
JESUS—HIS CROSS
   Our Promise of Life Forever
JESUS—HIS RESURRECTION
   Our Shared Triumph
JESUS—HIS RETURN
   Our Daily Hope

Jesus—His Birth

Our Pre-announced Gift From God

Hark! the herald angels sing,
"Glory to the new-born King,
Peace on earth, and mercy mild,
God and sinners reconciled!"

CHARLES WESLEY

In God's perfect timing His gift of Jesus was born to a despairing world—in God's perfect place. In the Church of the Holy Sepulchre in Jerusalem there is a spot that is pointed out to visitors as being "the center of the world." Nearby in Bethlehem, in a squalid stable, the Son of God was born. When men's hearts and souls most needed it, from out of the heart and mind of God came the Messiah.

A Saviour had been prophesied down through the ages. Men had sung songs predicting His coming. Surely their King would appear clothed in robes of great majesty—not wrapped in swaddling clothes, lying in a humble manger. How very different it all was, from what had been expected.

Most of us as children loved to hear the story of Jesus' birth. Christmas was such a wonderful time. As we excitedly anticipated all the gifts we were going to receive on Christmas Day, the reality of its real meaning seemed to get lost. It will always elude us until, by faith, we receive the Saviour and come to know Jesus. God's immeasurable love, reaching out to all mankind, is His gift to us.

Just before my younger son was born, I read that it is a good idea to give any older children a present when the new baby comes home from the hospital, so that the older children feel especially loved also. We gave such a gift to my three-year-old son, when we brought his new brother home. He was delighted and kept saying, "Isn't it nice of him to bring me a present!" He played with the gift, a toy garage—twice as big as his brother—and accepted the baby immediately into our family and into his heart.

When Jesus was born, God sent in Him a very special gift to show us how much *we* are loved. God's gift of salvation was only begun in that manger. This baby was a marked man, for He came to die for you and me. His gift was completed through His death and Resurrection. Now it is ours to receive.

Gifts should always be given through a heart of love, as God's was to us. The Wise Men came to adore the baby Jesus and their gifts of gold, frankincense, and myrrh represented the finest they could give their Saviour and Lord.

Just as these men gave gifts we too, no matter what our circumstances, can give Jesus Christ the best in our lives. For gold, we can give the kingship of our money to Him; for frankincense, we can give the worship of our dedicated lives; for myrrh, the symbol of bitterness and suffering, we can share in His sorrows and the world's.

—J. W. B.

For unto us a child is born, unto us a son
is given: and the government shall be upon
his shoulder: and his name shall be called
Wonderful, Counsellor, The mighty God,
The everlasting Father, The Prince of Peace.

Isaiah 9:6

Seven hundred years before Jesus was born, the prophet Isaiah saw him coming . . . Isaiah saw that this child was unique; he was "born" and he was "given." In other words, this child was both God and man! As God, he was given—the Father's love-gift to a sinful world. This child would be God in human flesh!

What would this child do? He would grow up and one day take the government of mankind upon his shoulder and bring order and peace to a world filled with confusion and war. But before taking the government upon his shoulder, he would first take a cross upon his shoulder, and then die upon that cross, bearing in his body the sins of the world. Before he could wear the diadem of glory as King of kings, he had to wear a shameful crown of thorns and give his life as a sacrifice for the sins of the world. The kingly Lion of the tribe of Judah first had to come as the lowly Lamb of God, for until sin had been paid for, God's righteous government could not be established.

WARREN W. WIERSBE

HIS NAME IS WONDERFUL

His Name is Wonderful,
His Name is Wonderful,
His Name is Wonderful,
Jesus my Lord.

He is the mighty King,
Master of ev'rything,
His Name is Wonderful,
Jesus my Lord.

He's the Great Shepherd,
The Rock of all Ages,
Almighty God is He.

Bow down before Him,
Love and adore Him.
His Name is Wonderful,
Jesus my Lord.

AUDREY MIEIR

The time draws near the birth of Christ.
The moon is hid, the night is still;
The Christmas bells from hill to hill
Answer each other in the mist.

Four voices of four hamlets round,
From far and near, on mead and moor,
Swell out and fail, as if a door
Were shut between me and the sound;

Each voice four changes on the wind,
That now dilate, and now decrease,
Peace and goodwill, goodwill and peace,
Peace and goodwill, to all mankind.

ALFRED TENNYSON
In Memoriam

LUKE 2:1–12

At that time Emperor Augustus ordered a census to be taken through-out the Roman Empire. When this first census took place, Quirinius was the governor of Syria. Everyone, then, went to register himself, each to his own home town.

Joseph went from the town of Nazareth in Galilee to the town of Bethlehem in Judea, the birthplace of King David. Joseph went there because he was a descendant of David. He went to register with Mary, who was promised in marriage to him. She was pregnant, and while they were in Bethlehem, the time came for her to have her baby. She gave birth to her first son, wrapped him in cloths and laid him in a manger—there was no room for them to stay in the inn.

There were some shepherds in that part of the country who were spending the night in the fields, taking care of their flocks. An angel of the Lord appeared to them, and the glory of the Lord shone over them. They were terribly afraid, but the angel said to them, "Don't be afraid! I am here with good news for you, which will bring great joy to all the people. This very day in David's town your Savior was born—Christ the Lord! And this is what will prove it to you: you will find a baby wrapped in cloths and lying in a manger."

GOOD NEWS

Her head was down, and he could not see her face. In fear, he asked her to name what he could do. She said to go outside and tend the fire and heat more water and to remain there until she called him. The animals watched him go, and they watched impassively as Mary sank to the straw.

The fire outside burned brightly in the southerly breeze and little trains of ruddy sparks flew off into the dark night. Joseph sat beside it, heating the water and praying.

No one came down from the inn to ask how the young woman felt. If she prayed, no one heard except the animals, some of whom stopped chewing for a moment to watch; others of whom opened sleepy eyes to see. Time was slow; there was an infinity of silence; a timeless time when the future of mankind hung in empty space . . . .

"Joseph." It was a soft call, but he heard it. At once, he picked up the second jar of water and hurried inside. The two lamps still shed a soft glow over the stable, even though it seemed years since they had been lighted.

The first thing he noticed was his wife. Mary was sitting tailor-fashion with her back against a manger wall. Her face was clean; her hair had been brushed. There were blue hollows under her eyes. She smiled at her husband and nodded. Then she stood.

She beckoned him to come closer. Joseph, mouth agape, followed her to a little manger. It had been cleaned but, where the animals had nipped the edges of the wood, the boards were worn and splintered. In the manger were the broad bolts of white swaddling she had brought on the trip. They were doubled underneath and over the top of the baby.

Mary smiled at her husband as he bent far over to look. There, among the cloths, he saw the tiny red face of an infant. This, said Joseph to himself, is the one of whom the angel spoke. He dropped to his knees beside the manger. This was the Messiah.

JIM BISHOP

CHRISTMAS EVERYWHERE

> Everywhere, everywhere, Christmas tonight!
> Christmas in lands of the fir-tree and pine,
> Christmas in lands of the palm-tree and vine,
> Christmas where snow-peaks stand solemn and white,
> Christmas where cornfields stand sunny and bright,
> Everywhere, everywhere, Christmas tonight!
>
> Christmas where children are hopeful and gay,
> Christmas where old men are patient and gray,
> Christmas where peace like a dove in his flight,
> Broods o'er brave men in the thick of the fight;
> Everywhere, everywhere, Christmas tonight!
>
> For the Christ-child who comes is the Master of all;
> No palace too great, no cottage too small . . . .

PHILLIPS BROOKS

Christ is the great central fact in the world's history. To Him everything looks forward or backward. All the lines of history converge upon Him. All the great purposes of God culminate in Him. The greatest and most momentous fact which the history of the world records is the fact of His birth.

CHARLES H. SPURGEON

THE CHRISTMAS SYMBOL

Only a manger, cold and bare,
  Only a maiden mild,
Only some shepherds kneeling there,
  Watching a little Child;
And yet that maiden's arms enfold
  The King of heaven above;
And in the Christ-Child we behold
  The Lord of Life and Love.

Only an altar high and fair,
  Only a white-robed priest,
Only Christ's children kneeling there
  Keeping the Christmas feast;
And yet beneath the outward sign
  The inward Grace is given—
His Presence, who is Lord Divine
  And King of earth and heaven.

                                   AUTHOR UNKNOWN

The shadow of the Cross fell over every detail of the Life of Christ from the beginning. It fell across His Crib. His Baptism was not just a call to teach, but to be the Victim prophesied by Isaiah; it was the whole burden of Satan's temptation on the Mount; it was hinted in the cleansing of the Temple when He challenged His enemies to destroy the Temple of His Body on Good Friday and He would rebuild it on Easter; it was hidden in the title of "Savior" He accepted when He forgave a prostitute's sins; it was implied in the Beatitudes, for anyone who would practice the Beatitudes in this world would be crucified; it was prophesied clearly three times as He gave details of His Death and Resurrection; it was hidden in the seven times He used the word "Hour" in contrast to "Day" which stood for His conquest of evil.

Finally, the Cross met its defeat when the earth received its most serious wound—the empty Tomb. To create the world cost God nothing; to save it from sin cost His Life Blood.

                                   FULTON J. SHEEN

The cross always stands near the manger.

                                   AMY CARMICHAEL

He turned and looked a moment at the manger. "This is our cross, Mary. Yours and mine—for you know how much I love him too. But this is our cross—to know that our son's hour will come and we can't stop it. To live with that certainty every day of our lives. But this is our blessing," he told her. "To know that in his living and his dying he will be lifting the yoke somewhat for all men. Life with its burdens will be more tolerable. There will be hope. Not only for the freedom of Israel, our own people, but all people who are enslaved.

"And hope for the tormented spirit, Mary. To have some link, some proof that the God we worship really cares about us. Not to have to *fight* God any more, not to be estranged from him." Joseph's face was working, he was struggling to make it clear. "That too is suffering, perhaps the worst suffering of all. Somehow through this child all this will come about."

MARJORIE HOLMES

THE SHEPHERD SPEAKS

Out of the midnight sky a great dawn broke,
And a voice singing flooded us with song.
"In David's city was He born," it sang.
"A Saviour, Christ the Lord." The while I sat
Shivering with the thrill of that great cry,
A mighty choir a thousandfold more sweet
Suddenly sang, "Glory to God, and Peace—
Peace on the earth"; my heart, almost unnerved
By that swift loveliness, would hardly beat.
Speechless we waited till the accustomed night
Gave us no promise more of sweet surprise;
Then scrambling to our feet, without a word
We started through the fields to find the Child.

JOHN ERSKINE

AWAY IN A MANGER

Away in a manger, no crib for a bed,
The little Lord Jesus laid down His sweet head.
The stars in the bright sky looked down where He lay,
The little Lord Jesus, asleep on the hay.

The cattle are lowing, the baby awakes,
But little Lord Jesus, no crying He makes.

I love Thee, Lord Jesus! Look down from the sky,
And stay by my side until morning is nigh.

Be near me, Lord Jesus! I ask Thee to stay
Close by me forever, and love me, I pray.
Bless all the dear children in Thy tender care,
And fit us for heaven, to live with Thee there.

> MARTIN LUTHER
> Stanzas 1, 2
> JOHN THOMAS MC FARLAND
> Stanza 3

The Bible is the cradle in which Christ lies.

> MARTIN LUTHER

This is the month, and this the happy morn,
Wherein the Son of Heaven's eternal King,
Of wedded maid and virgin mother born,
Our great redemption from above did bring;
For so the holy sages once did sing,
  That He our deadly forfeit should release;
And with His Father work us a perpetual peace . . . .

> JOHN MILTON
> *On the Morning of Christ's Nativity*

If Christ is born a thousand times in
Bethlehem and not in thee, then art thou
lost for ever.

> ANGELUS SILESIUS

INCARNATE LOVE

Love came down at Christmas,
  Love all lovely, Love Divine;
Love was born at Christmas,
  Star and Angels gave the sign.

Worship we the Godhead,
  Love incarnate, Love Divine;
Worship we our Jesus:
  But wherewith for sacred sign?

Love shall be our token,
  Love be yours and Love be mine,
Love to God and all men,
  Love for plea and gift and sign.
                              CHRISTINA G. ROSSETTI

The blessedness of Christmas is all wrapped up in the Person of Jesus. Our relationship determines the measure of the blessing.
                              AUTHOR UNKNOWN

CHRISTMAS

The snow is full of silver light
Spilled from the heavens' tilted cup
And, on this holy, tranquil night,
The eyes of men are lifted up
To see the promise written fair,
The hope of peace for all on earth,
And hear the singing bells declare
The marvel of the dear Christ's birth.
The way from year to year is long
And though the road be dark so far,
Bright is the manger, sweet the song,
The steeple rises to the Star.
                              FAITH BALDWIN

I never realized God's birth before,
How he grew likest God in being born.

  .   .   .   .   .   .

Such ever was love's way—to rise, it stoops.
                              ROBERT BROWNING

CHRISTMAS EVE

The door is on the latch tonight,
  The hearth-fire is aglow,
I seem to hear soft passing feet—
  The Christ child in the snow.

My heart is open wide tonight
For stranger, kith or kin.
I would not bar a single door
Where Love might enter in.
KATE DOUGLAS WIGGIN

THE INN THAT MISSED ITS CHANCE

(*The Landlord Speaks*, A.D. 28)

Of course, if I had known them, who they were,
And who was He that should be born that night—
For now I learn that they will make Him King,
A second David, who will ransom us
From these Philistine Romans—who but He
That feeds an army with a loaf of bread,
And if a soldier falls, He touches him
And up he leaps, uninjured? Had I known,
I would have turned the whole inn upside down,
His honor, Marcus Lucius, and the rest,
And sent them all to stables, had I known.
So you have seen Him, stranger, and perhaps
Again may see Him? Prithee say for me,
I did not know; and if He comes again
As He will surely come, with retinue,
And banners, and an army, tell my Lord
That all my inn is His to make amends.

Alas! Alas! to miss a chance like that!
This inn might be the chief among them all,
The birthplace of Messiah, had I known!
AMOS RUSSEL WELLS

If the inhabitants of Bethlehem had known who Joseph and Mary were and who the little child was who would be born of her—how gladly would they have prepared a little place for Him! But as it was then, it often is today. Many leave the Saviour, who is knocking, standing at the door of their heart, without paying attention to Him. For they have no place for Jesus. Many are too busy with themselves, and do not believe that He is the Son of the living God . . . .

It is told that Victoria, the Queen of England, when staying at her summer residence *Balmoral*, likes to take long walks through the woods in simple clothes, and has pleasure in remaining unknown. Some years ago, she was caught in a heavy rainstorm while on one of these trips.

Noticing an old cottage, she ran towards it for refuge. In this cottage lived an old peasant woman alone, who left her house only to take care of her goat and tend her small garden.

The Queen greeted her and kindly asked if she could borrow an umbrella. She added that she would take care to have it returned soon to its owner. The old woman had never seen the Queen, and so she had no idea who she could be.

Therefore she answered in a grudging tone, "Well, I have two umbrellas. One is very good and almost new. I have used it very little. The other one is very worn and has had its time. You may take the old one; the new one I don't lend to anybody—for who knows whether I would ever get it back?" With these words, she gave the Queen the old umbrella, which was torn and battered with spokes sticking out on all sides.

The Queen thought, *With this kind of weather, a bad umbrella is better than nothing at all,* and accepted it politely. Thanking the woman, she left smiling.

But how great was the horror of the poor old woman, when the next morning, a servant in royal livery entered and returned to her the old umbrella in the name of Queen Victoria—with her thanks—and the assurance that Her Majesty had received good service from it! How sorry she was that she had not offered to the Queen the very best she had, and over and over she cried out, "If only I had known! Oh, if only I would have known!"

This will also be the cry of those who will realize too late who *He* is in the day when all eyes will see Him.

CASPER TEN BOOM
Corrie's Christmas Memories

Were earth a thousand times as fair,
Beset with gold and jewels rare,
She yet were far too poor to be
A narrow cradle, Lord, for Thee.

MARTIN LUTHER

BEFORE THE PALING OF THE STARS

Before the paling of the stars,
　Before the winter morn,
Before the earliest cockcrow,
　Jesus Christ was born:
Born in a stable,
　Cradled in a manger,
In the world His hands had made
　Born a stranger.

Priest and king lay fast asleep
　In Jerusalem,
Young and old lay fast asleep
　In crowded Bethlehem;
Saint and Angel, ox and ass,
　Kept a watch together
Before the Christmas daybreak
　In the winter weather.

Jesus on His mother's breast
　In the stable cold,
Spotless Lamb of God was He,
　Shepherd of the fold:
Let us kneel with Mary maid,
　With Joseph bent and hoary,
With Saint and Angel, ox and ass,
　To hail the King of Glory.

CHRISTINA G. ROSSETTI

Jesus came to save his people from sin. That's the meaning of the name he was given. "You shall call his name Jesus, for he will save his people from their sins." He was Immanuel, God with us. He came not to establish the traditions of a new religion but to get to the inner heart of people's need. His life, message, death and resurrection were to reconcile us with God eternally. And that wondrous process for each of us begins in the healing of our inner selves. Our memories are liberated with forgiveness, our personalities are reformed around the person of Christ himself, our turbulent drives and needs are satisfied and reordered around his guidance and direction. The heart becomes his home.

"The Father and I will make our home in you." The Christmas carol suddenly has meaning, "Where meek souls will receive him still, the dear Christ enters in." Then we can sing, "O come to us, abide with us, O Christ, Immanuel."

LLOYD JOHN OGILVIE
Life Without Limits

This is Christmas—the real meaning of it.

God loving; searching; giving himself—to us.

Man needing; receiving; giving himself—to God.

Redemption's glorious exchange of gifts! Without which we cannot live; without which we cannot give to those we love anything of lasting value.

This is the meaning of Christmas—the wonder and the glory of it.

RUTH BELL GRAHAM
"This Too I Shall Give"

FOR CHRISTMAS THE YEAR ROUND

O come to my heart, Lord Jesus,
There is room in my heart for Thee.

Lord Jesus, we thank Thee for the spirit shed abroad in human hearts on Christmas. Even as we invited Thee on Christmas to be born again in our hearts, so wilt Thou now go with us throughout the days ahead, to be our Companion in all that we do. Wilt Thou help each one of us to keep Christmas alive in our hearts and in our homes, that it may continue to glow, to shed its warmth, to speak its message during all the bleak days of winter.

May we hold to that spirit, that we may be as gentle and as kindly today as we were on Christmas Eve, as generous tomorrow as we were on Christmas morning.

Then if—by Thy help—we should live through a whole week in that spirit, it may be we can go into another week, and thus be encouraged and gladdened by the discovery that Christmas can last the year round.

So give us joyful, cheerful hearts to the glory of Jesus Christ, our Lord, Amen.

PETER MARSHALL
The Prayers of Peter Marshall

Now all this was done, that it might be fulfilled which was spoken of the Lord by the prophet, saying,

Behold, a virgin shall be with child, and shall bring forth a son, and they shall call his name Emmanuel, which being interpreted is, God with us.

Matthew 1:22, 23

To think, Lord Jesus, You would leave the glory of Your heavenly home to come as a little baby, born in such a humble manger, to give us the most magnificent gift that anyone could receive—the gift of God's love and redemption. May my life, my heart, be a worthy gift for You. Amen.

—J. W. B.

Jesus—His Life and Ministry

Our Divine Example

The influence of His life, His words, and His death, have, from the first, been like leaven cast into the mass of humanity.

CUNNINGHAM GEIKIE

At the time of Jesus' life on earth, the world was racked by injustice, hatred, and confusion—just as it is today. But as He went about the countryside, His love and caring changed people, gave them new natures, a new hope. He taught that each person is precious to God. "The very hairs of your head are all numbered" (Matthew 10:30). To those who were ready to listen and accept the Son of God's teachings, His example inspired people everywhere He went.

The call He gave to His disciples is still heard today. It was this call that inspired Mother Teresa of Calcutta to leave the comfort of her home and travel to India to work among the most destitute of all—the emaciated, rotting shells of people dying in the streets. This ministry can only be brought about, as she works amongst the stench and horror of these dear souls, by the love of Jesus Christ in this amazing woman's life.

Florence Nightingale, years before, had heard the same call and had gone to the carnage of the battlefields of the Boer War to give tender and loving aid to the wounded and dying. "We are His glory, when we follow His ways," she said.

Not all of us are called to minister far from home. Around us in our communities are people who need Him. Our compassion, brought about by His Holy Spirit, can reach out to those who have lost hope and who desperately seek an answer to their seemingly unsolvable problems. Ministering through Him we avoid the ego trip that can so easily become our incentive, instead of wanting to glorify Him.

His hand is still reaching out to transform lives. He takes us, even if our faith is as small as "a grain of mustard seed," then helps us grow each day to the full beauty of discipleship.

I often wonder what His thoughts must have been the day He left His home in Nazareth for the last time, to face an angry, hostile world on a mission He knew He had been born for—to die for us. But until that time, three years later, He would accomplish more than any man has ever done in a whole lifetime.

So little is written of Jesus' life before He began those three power-packed years of His ministry. The account of His life in the Gospels is sketchy. What a beautiful child He must have been! Playing with His friends in the fields around His home; loving nature, which would be used to illustrate His parables in the years to come. As He worked with Joseph in the carpenter's shop did He think—as He picked up the nails and hammered them into the wood—of that day when His hands would be pierced by nails as they stretched Him on a Cross?

—J. W. B.

And the child grew, and waxed strong in
spirit, filled with wisdom: And the grace of
God was upon him.

Luke 2:40

Somehow I always picture the boy Jesus as a sturdy, strong, barefoot lad with cheeks and arms kissed by the sun. With coal black hair and piercing bright eyes He was a picture of eager youth and energetic vigor. No doubt in company with other boys His age He climbed and explored all the hills that surrounded Nazareth like a giant amphitheater. There He watched the wind blowing the wild flowers. He followed the hill farmers as they raked their hay and harvested their grain. He stealthily stalked the wild foxes and found their secret dens. He came across bird nests in the shrubby hedgerows and trees. Perhaps once or twice He picked up a fallen fledgling from the ground, tenderly replacing it in its nest.

The sights and sounds familiar to the Galilean countryside were some of the fine fabric woven into His early years. They obviously made an enormous impression on Him. Later in life when He spoke profound and imperishable truth in common layman's language it was always couched in terms of trees and grass, seed and soil, sparrows and foxes, vineyards and vinedressers, weeds and wheat, wind and weather.

W. PHILLIP KELLER
Rabboni

In May 1882, in Edinburgh, Scotland, the Reverend Walter J. Mathams had just returned from a visit to the Holy Land. He was deeply moved by his experiences there and said, "I went through this Land with vivid scenes of Christ and the children amongst the flowers and birds. I saw Him as the living Christ for all children of all lands and ages. Not 'above the bright blue sky,' but here on the dusty road of human life. I saw Him then and I see Him now, leading all His lambs toward the infinite life. A very present Help is He."

Shortly after his return from the Holy Land, Mathams wrote the children's hymn "Jesus, Friend of Little Children."

> Jesus, Friend of little children,
>   Be a friend to me;
> Take my hand and ever keep me,
>   Close to Thee.
>
> Teach me how to grow in goodness,
>   Daily as I grow;
> Thou hast been a child,
>   And surely Thou dost know.
>
> Never leave me, nor forsake me,
>   Ever be my Friend;
> For I need Thee, from life's dawning
>   To its end.
>
> WALTER J. MATHAMS

The original version of Isaac Watts' great hymn was true to fact:

> When I survey the wondrous Cross,
> Where *the young Prince* of glory died.

And no one has ever understood the heart of youth, in its gaiety and gallantry and generosity and hope, its sudden loneliness and haunting dreams and hidden conflicts and strong temptations, no one has understood it nearly so well as Jesus. And no one ever realised more clearly than Jesus did that the adolescent years of life, when strange dormant thoughts are stirring and the whole world begins to unfold, are God's best chance with the soul. When Jesus and youth come together, deep calls to deep. There is an immediate, instinctive feeling of kinship, and everything that is fine and noble and pure in youth bows down in admiration and adoration before Him.

> JAMES S. STEWART

Judean hills are holy,
Judean hills are fair,
For one can find the footprints
Of Jesus, everywhere.

WILLIAM L. STIDGER

Jesus made plain in his life how dear to him was the beauty of the world. He loved to wander by the lake, among the corn, and on the grassy hills. He marked the aspects of the beauty of flowers. He loved animals, and drew some of his loveliest teaching from their ways. When weary, he sought the hilltop by night; when uplifted by strong communion, the higher ridges of Hermon; when exceeding sorrowful, the lonely olive grove.

STOPFORD BROOKE

JESUS THE CARPENTER

If I could hold within my hand
  The hammer Jesus swung,
Not all the gold in all the land,
Nor jewels countless as the sand,
  All in the balance flung,
Could weigh the value of that thing
Round which His fingers once did cling.

If I could have the table Christ
  Once made in Nazareth,
Not all the pearls in all the sea,
Nor crowns of kings or kings to be
  As long as men have breath,
Could buy that thing of wood He made—
The Lord of Lords who learned a trade.

Yea, but His hammer still is shown
  By honest hands that toil,
And round His table men sit down;

> And all are equals, with a crown
> Nor gold nor pearls can soil;
> The shop of Nazareth was bare—
> But brotherhood was builded there.
>
> CHARLES M. SHELDON

In His daily toil of handling, hewing, and shaping the tough wild olive wood and hard acacia common to the region, He developed tough sinews and hard muscles. He knew what weariness and work and sweat and strain took from a man.

In buying His lumber and selling His finished yokes, plows, chests, tables, benches, and candlesticks, He had to barter or deal in hard cash. He was exposed to all the whims of a busy, boisterous, brutal world. Amid that world He came to be known as *the carpenter of Nazareth*. If one wanted excellent workmanship at an honest price, he went to Jesus. His craftsmanship was first class. His price was right. But best of all He loved people and could become your friend.

Then quietly one spring day He laid down His tools. He dusted off His strong hands. He walked out of the shop never to return to it again.

> W. PHILLIP KELLER
> *Rabboni*

> And it came to pass in those days, that Jesus came from Nazareth of Galilee, and was baptized of John in Jordan. And straightway coming up out of the water, he saw the heavens opened, and the Spirit like a dove descending upon him: And there came a voice from heaven, saying, Thou art my beloved Son, in whom I am well pleased.
>
> Mark 1:9–11

When you see the sinless Christ going to the sinners' baptism, you are seeing love going to a great redeeming act of self-identification. It was a prophecy of what the coming years were to bring, when the Lord of glory was to earn the name "Friend of publicans and sinners," to go where need called, reckless of His reputation, to sit often at outcasts' tables, and to die at last between two thieves. "He was numbered with the transgressors" (Isaiah 53:12). True, but He numbered Himself with them first of all. At the Jordan, Jesus took His shame, their trouble His trouble, their penitence His penitence, their burden His burden. It was the beginning of the work that was crowned at Calvary, when He carried the burden away for ever.

Hence the baptism of Jesus points the fact that the only love which can ever possess redeeming power is a love that goes all the way and identifies itself with others. So Moses, in the day of his people's sin, stood and cried—"Blot me, I pray thee, out of thy book [of life] which thou hast written" (Exodus 32:32). So Paul, lamenting the blindness of his nation, exclaimed—"I could wish that myself were accursed from Christ for my brethren, my kinsmen according to the flesh" (Romans 9:3). George Fox prayed "to be baptised" (note the word) "into a sense of all conditions, that I might know the needs and feel the sorrows of all." Father Damien's self-identification meant literal leprosy. "Whenever I preach to my people," he said, "I do not say, 'my brethren,' as you do, but 'we lepers.' People pity me and think me unfortunate, but I think myself the happiest of missionaries." "Do you think that I care for my soul if my boy be gone to the fire?" cries the mother in Tennyson's *Rizpah*. It is that same self-identifying love of which Jesus' baptism speaks.

JAMES S. STEWART

And Jesus returned in the power of the Spirit into Galilee: and there went out a fame of him through all the region round about. And he taught in their synagogues, being glorified of all. And he came to Nazareth, where he had been brought up: and, as his custom was, he went into the synagogue on the sabbath day, and stood up for to read. And there was delivered unto him the book of the prophet Esaias [Isaiah]. And when he had opened the book, he found the place where it was written, The Spirit of the Lord is upon me, because he hath anointed me to preach the gospel to the poor; he hath sent me to heal the brokenhearted, to preach deliverance to the captives, and recovering of sight to the blind, to set at liberty them that are bruised, To preach the acceptable year of the Lord. And he closed the book, and he gave it again to the minister, and sat down. And the eyes of all them that were in the synagogue were fastened on him. And he began to say unto them, This day is this scripture fulfilled in your ears. And all bare him witness, and wondered at the gracious words which proceeded out of his mouth . . . .

Luke 4:14–22

In God's sight a person is the most precious of all values. This truth possessed Jesus and never let Him go. He thought it, taught it, and lived it with full devotion. He illustrated it with stories of the lost sheep, the lost coin, and the lost son.

Every individual is inherently worthful to the Father—every child everywhere, of every race, of every condition. Love requires response, and parenthood craves companionship and cooperation. Therefore every human being on this globe is indispensable to God, indispensable in the sense that God can never be fully Himself without loving comradeship, and He can never complete His work without faithful cooperation from every individual everywhere.

Jesus taught and lived the twin truths that man needs God and God needs man, which is to say, parents and child are so bound together that cleavage is disastrous. No idea could be further from the mind of our Lord than the persistent doctrine that God is so transcendent, so holy, so sovereign that He is unknowable, inaccessible, and unresponsive. In the prayer which He taught His disciples, Jesus makes it clear that men should carry all their needs to the Father, even a petition for the satisfaction of daily bodily requirements. Jesus knew men to be frail, sinful, easily corrupted, sometimes monstrously depraved, capable of cruel and atrocious behavior—but always, always, always a child of God, and, even when a prodigal, indispensable to the lonely and yearning heart of the Father.

KIRBY PAGE

I saw a stranger yestreen;
I put food in the eating place,
Drink in the drinking place,
Music in the listening place,
And, in the sacred name of the Father,
He blessed myself and my house,
My cattle and my dear ones.
And the lark sang in her song,
    Often, often, often,
Goes the Christ in the stranger's guise;
    Often, often, often,
Goes the Christ in the stranger's guise.
Ancient Gaelic poem

If you will study the history of Christ's ministry from Baptism to Ascension, you will discover that it is mostly made up of little words, little deeds, little prayers, little sympathies, adding themselves together in unwearied succession. The Gospel is full of divine attempts to help and heal, in body, mind, and heart, individual men. The completed beauty of Christ's life is only the added beauty of little inconspicuous acts of beauty—talking with the woman at the well; going far up into the North country to talk with the Syrophenician woman; showing the young ruler the stealthy ambition laid away in his heart that kept him out of the kingdom of Heaven; shedding a tear at the grave of Lazarus; teaching a little knot of followers how to pray; preaching the Gospel one Sunday afternoon to two disciples going out to Emmaus; kindling a fire and broiling fish that His disciples might have a breakfast waiting for them when they came ashore from a night of fishing, cold, tired, and discouraged. All of these things, you see, let us in so easily into the real quality and tone of God's interest, so specific, so narrowed down, so enlisted in what is small, so engrossed with what is minute.

CHARLES H. PARKHURST

Do small things as if they were great, because of the majesty of Jesus Christ, who works them in us and who lives our life; and great things as small and easy, because of His omnipotence.

BLAISE PASCAL

We must believe in people as Jesus did. He showed faith in the most hopeless characters. He believed in those who were called "publicans and sinners." If we described them as "stand-over men and down-and-outs" it would probably conjure up a more exact picture of the kind of people with whom He chose to associate. Yet He did associate with them because He knew there was still good that could be called forth. He believed in rough, hard-swearing half-educated fishermen like Peter, James and John and made them the foundation of His Church. He believed in people who seemed to be incurably selfish like Zacchaeus and Matthew. He believed in people whose lives and whose mental health had been wrecked by lust, people like Mary of Magdala and the woman taken in sin. To such people He said, "Neither do I condemn you, go and sin no more." If He could accept people like that, surely you and I can accept people who sin against us!

More than that, if He believed that they could still do great things with their lives, as they did when inspired by Him, surely we can look for the buried treasure in the problem people we have to deal with and enter into the great Christian adventure of bringing forth that treasure. It probably only needs a little encouragement, a little faith, forbearance and forgiveness to produce wonderful results.

GORDON POWELL

If every person in the world had adequate food, housing, income; if all men were equal; if every possible social evil and injustice were done away with, men would still need one thing: Christ!

J. W. HYDE

hours and hours of little touches of brilliance
  in everyday history,
      mary and her perfume.
        paul and a song in jail.
          Jesus spending the afternoon with
              zacchaeus
or washing the tired feet of His followers
or simply holding a child
    on His lap.

ANN KIEMEL

A member of the New York Avenue Church, Washington, which Mr. Lincoln attended while living at the Capital, told me of a Sunday morning when Mr. Lincoln was in his pew and there happened up the aisle slowly an oldish man, evidently a stranger, waiting for an usher to find a seat for him in the crowded church. He paused every two or three steps after getting well forward and then turned to walk back. Just as he was passing Mr. Lincoln's pew (now marked with his name), Mr. Lincoln stretched out that long arm of his and said to the stranger:

"Come in here with me."

With the greatest war the nation had (up to that time) upon his hands and heart, he never lost sight of individual needs, and big and great as he was, he never failed to stretch out a helping hand to do even little things.

There is an imperishable influence in the lives of such as try every day to do good in ways either large or small.

JOHN WANAMAKER

Since my heart was touched at seven-
teen, I believe I have never awakened from
sleep, in sickness or in health, by day or by
night, without my first waking thought
being how best I might serve my Lord.

ELIZABETH FRY
(*English Victorian prison reformer*)

It was after World War II and I was working in East Germany, teaching the Gospel in a huge cathedral. I went into a counseling area to talk with people individually; there were many more who needed help waiting outside in another room. I heard a very noisy discussion, everyone seemed to be talking too loudly at the same time. Suddenly everything was quiet and I heard an unusually tender, beautiful voice singing . . . . "Out of my bondage, sorrow and night, Jesus, I come."

I opened the door into the room where the inquirers were waiting and saw a child of about fourteen years of age. Her face was like an angel, and there was something so moving about her that many in the room were crying. The girl's mother stood beside her and held her hand.

When they came into the inquiry room, I found out that the girl's name was Elsa, and I realized immediately that she was not a normal child.

"Where did you learn that song, Elsa?" I asked her gently.

"In prison . . . a man taught it to me, and I sang it every day."

"Why was Elsa in prison?" I asked her mother.

"My husband is a communist. Elsa is mentally retarded. She loves the Lord Jesus and speaks about Him frequently, but her father is an atheist and a leader in his party, so he had no difficulty putting Elsa in prison. A short while ago we got her out . . . it was so terribly cold in that jail that the guards themselves helped me get Elsa out. They heard and enjoyed her singing, and Elsa was always ready to tell them about her Lord."

My lips quivered as I held Elsa's hands, and I remembered so many things . . . the Bible studies in Holland . . . and what Father had often said to me. "Corrie, what you do among these people is of little importance in the eyes of men, but I'm sure in God's eyes it is the most valuable work of all."

CORRIE TEN BOOM
In My Father's House

Consider Jesus of Nazareth, the most generous-hearted person who ever lived. He never refused a request for help. Great multitudes followed Him, and He healed them all. He went out of His way to cross racial and religious barriers. He compassed the whole world in His love.

AUTHOR UNKNOWN

A young doctor was turning the lights out in a mission hall, where he had been working in the East End of London, when he found a small, dirty little boy. The lad begged the doctor to let him sleep there as he had nowhere else to go. The boy told him that he had been living in a coal bunker with some other boys. As the doctor won the confidence of the child, he persuaded him to show him where the place was. After going through many dark alleys, they came to a hole in a wall that was part of a factory. Crawling through, the doctor found thirteen boys huddled under rags to keep them warm. All were asleep.

Because of this experience the doctor's heart was burdened by the Lord to start a home in London for abandoned children. When he died, Dr. Thomas J. Barnardo had founded homes for over eighty thousand homeless boys and girls. This work started when he saw one small child without a place to sleep. In each town or city where we live there is still a need that Christ wants *us* to reach out and touch in His name. Are we willing to open our hearts?

O Master, let me walk with Thee
In lowly paths of service free;
Tell me Thy secret; help me bear
The strain of toil, the fret of care.

Help me the slow of heart to move
By some clear, winning word of love;
Teach me the wayward feet to stay,
And guide them in the homeward way.

Teach me Thy patience; still with Thee
In closer, dearer company,
In work that keeps faith sweet and strong,
In trust that triumphs over wrong;

In hope that sends a shining ray
Far down the future's broadening way;
In peace that only Thou canst give,
With Thee, O Master, let me live.

WASHINGTON GLADDEN

I am to become a Christ to my neighbor
and be for him what Christ is for me.

MARTIN LUTHER

Have you ever noticed how much of Christ's life was spent in doing kind things—in merely doing kind things? Run over it with that in view, and you will find that He spent a great proportion of His time simply in making people happy, in doing good turns to people. There is only one thing greater than happiness in the world, and that is holiness; and it is not in our keeping; but what God has put in our power is the happiness of those about us; that is largely to be secured by our being kind to them.

HENRY DRUMMOND

And [Christ] saw two ships standing by
the lake: but the fisherman were gone out
of them, and were washing their nets.

Luke 5:2

They were washing their nets after a long night of fishing. There was very little to wash out of their nets, because they hadn't caught anything in them!

I can imagine that Peter did not enjoy the fact of his failure. He was a successful man. He was a man of some financial standing. He was not a novice fisherman. He was adept at his work, but he had failed that night.

Christ got into Peter's boat and asked to be taken a little way out from land so He could speak to the crowd that had ". . . pressed upon him to hear the word of God . . ." (Luke 5:1).

What could He teach from the boat of a fisherman who had failed to catch fish? We think success is the only podium. I have tried to bargain with Him by saying, "Promote me, Lord, and I'll glorify You from the pinnacle." He has replied, "Glorify Me where you are, or you'll never glorify Me at all."

JEANNETTE CLIFT

TO THE END

O Jesus, I have promised
  To serve Thee to the end;
Be Thou forever near me,
  My Master and my Friend;
I shall not fear the battle
  If Thou art by my side,
Nor wander from the pathway
  If Thou wilt be my Guide.

JOHN E. BODE

It is His face that will hold your gaze—and will haunt you long after the sun has gone down, and the purple night, cool and starlit, has stilled every noise in the city, while only the Syrian stars wink unsleeping.

One is aware of that face even in such a crowd. Having once seen it, one sees it everywhere, for it is a haunting face—an expression that will not fade . . . eyes whose fires never die out . . . a face that lingers in memory. Farmers were to see it as they followed the swaying plow, and fishermen were to watch it dancing on the sun-flecked water.

This One who walks like a king is named Jesus. They called Him the Nazarene or the Galilean. He called Himself the Son of Man.

The common people speak of Him softly, with deep affection, such as the shepherds know, who carry the little lambs in their bosoms.

The beggars whisper His name in the streets as they pass, and the children may be heard singing about Him. His name has been breathed in prayer and whispered at night under the stars. He is known to the diseased, the human flotsam and jetsam that shuffles in and out of the towns and drifts hopelessly along the dusty highways of human misery.

His fame has trickled down to the streets of forgotten men, has seeped into the shadowed refuges of the unremembered women. It is Jesus of Nazareth.

Any outcast could tell you of Him. There are women whose lives have been changed who could tell you of Him—but not without tears. There are silent men—walking strangely as if unaccustomed to it—who speak of Him with lights in their eyes.

It is Jesus whom they are crowding to see. They want to look on His face to see the quality of His expression that seems to promise so much

to the weary and the heavy-laden; that look that seems to offer healing of
mind and soul and body;
 forgiveness of sin;
  another chance—a beginning again.
 His look seemed to sing of tomorrow—a new tomorrow—in which
there should be no more pain
     no more suffering
    nor persecution
   nor cruelty
  nor hunger
  nor neglect
 nor disillusionments
nor broken promises
nor death.

PETER MARSHALL
"The Touch of Faith"

Him evermore I behold
Walking in Galilee,
Through the cornfield's waving gold,
In hamlet or grassy wold,
By the shores of the Beautiful Sea.
He toucheth the sightless eyes;
Before Him the demons flee;
To the dead He sayeth: Arise!
To the living: Follow me!
And that voice still soundeth on
From the centuries that are gone,
To the centuries that shall be!

HENRY WADSWORTH LONGFELLOW

When Jesus healed the man blind from
birth, He let him grope his way, still blind,
to wash in the pool—and then the light
broke. We don't need to know what we're
groping toward—or why. It is enough that
we have Christ's direction. The light will
break in God's own time.

AUTHOR UNKNOWN

"What happened?"

"I met Jesus Christ."

"You what?"

"I met Jesus Christ. Before this I knew about Him, but now I know Him."

"If you tell me that you have had a vision . . . ."

"No, no vision. But I did meet Jesus Christ."

"I don't know whether you want to see me or not," I replied, "but I want to see you."

When she came to my office, my eye confirmed what my ear had led me to suspect. This was a "healed" person. I do not mean to detract one iota from the contribution they make to the lives of wounded human beings, but clinical psychology and psychiatry must not be allowed to pose as saviors or redeemers. Therapy can never be a substitute for a life of faith. I knew, from my training in psychology, that no reputable therapist could ever promise this kind of "cure," this new "wholeness." There is no plastic surgery to remove the psychological scars that all of us bear to some extent. By supportive psychotherapy we can be comforted and by reconstructive psychotherapy we can be somewhat readjusted, develop new coping mechanisms, but . . . we cannot be healed or cured. This woman, seated before me, expressing gratitude and claiming to have met Jesus, was "healed." She knew it, and I knew it.

JOHN POWELL

Jesus was not merely selfless; he was without self. He came "not to be ministered unto, but to minister." Jesus was selfless and therefore he was restful, because an adjustment to life that asks nothing for self always brings that happy result.

G. H. MORLING

Clinging to a slope at the northern tip of this Sea of Galilee is Bethsaida, and close by Bethsaida was the place where Jesus fed the five thousand. It was Andrew, "a local boy," who came to Jesus that day and said, "There is a lad here, which hath five barley loaves, and two small fishes . . ." (John 6:9). And He fed them. I used to wonder about that miracle when I was young and full of doubts—but no more, since He has fed me. Stop wondering! Isn't it enough to know that we can never get beyond His love and care?

And there's another thing to remember about this day of feeding: Jesus fed them with the help of a boy's hand. A hand like yours and mine. *Use my hand, Lord . . . .*

> Take my hands, and let them move
> At the impulse of thy love.

Use me and lead me, Master, lest someone die of hunger!

DALE EVANS ROGERS
Where He Leads

HIS COMPASSION

The miracles of Christ were, almost all of them, mere acts of benevolence. He was poor; He had neither raiment nor money to give; and yet there was suffering round about Him, and He relieved it. The miracles of Christ were never wrought in an ostentatious way. Never were they wrought for the purpose of exalting Himself. They were not employed by Him when arguments failed, to carry men away by superstitions and enthusiasm. Multitudes resorted to Him for help—the sick, the blind, the deaf, lepers, all kinds of unfortunate people; and miracles were His means of bestowing charity upon them. No hospital had He to which He could send them; He was His own hospital. His miracles were His general acts of kindness. As laid down in the Gospel they represent the heart of God.

HENRY WARD BEECHER

> Jesus was himself the one convincing
> and permanent miracle.

IAN MACLAREN

Jesus spoke, but he also healed. The two went together; they were the equipoise between loving God and loving one's neighbour—the two duties into which Jesus resolved all that the Law laid down and the prophets had proclaimed. Even in the Garden of Gethsemane he healed, restoring the man's ear that Peter had impulsively hacked off with his sword. For that matter, even on the Cross he offered healing words to the penitent thief crucified beside him, making a rendezvous with him in paradise. Jesus never for one moment forgot our human need for bodies and minds in working order; for eyes that truly see and ears that truly hear. His compassion for the maimed, whether they were physically, mentally or spiritually disabled, was fathomless.

MALCOLM MUGGERIDGE

In fancy I stood by the shore, one day,
  Of the beautiful murm'ring sea;
I saw the great crowds as they thronged the way
  Of the Stranger of Galilee.

I saw how the man who was blind from birth
  In a moment was made to see;
The lame were made whole by the matchless skill
  Of the Stranger of Galilee.

And I felt I could love Him forever,
  So gracious and tender was He!
I claim'd Him that day as my Saviour,
  This Stranger of Galilee.

                                        MRS. C. H. MORRIS

Hitherto have ye asked nothing in my
name: ask, and ye shall receive, that your
joy may be full.

                                        John 16:24

"Hitherto nothing." "In that day ye shall ask in My name and shall receive." (*See* John 16:24, 26.) These two conditions are still found in the Church. With the great majority of Christians there is such a lack of knowledge of their oneness with Christ Jesus, and of the Holy Spirit as the Spirit of prayer, that they do not even attempt to claim the wonderful promises Christ here gives. But where God's children know what it is to abide in Christ and in vital union with Him, and to yield to the Holy Spirit's teaching, they begin to learn that their intercession avails much, and that God will give the power of His Spirit in answer to their prayer.

It is faith in the power of Jesus' name, and in our right to use it, that will give us the courage to follow on where God invites us to the holy office of intercessors. When our Lord Jesus, in His farewell discourse, gave His unlimited prayer promise, He sent the disciples out into the world with this consciousness: "He who sits upon the throne, and who lives in my heart, has promised that what I ask in His name I shall receive. He will do it."

                                        ANDREW MURRAY

Only, O Lord, in Thy dear love
Fit us for perfect rest above;
And help us this and every day,
To live more nearly as we pray.
                    JOHN KEBLE

To pray is to let Jesus into our lives. He knocks and seeks admittance, not only in the solemn hours of secret prayer when you bend the knee or fold your hands in supplication, or when you hold fellowship with other Christians in a prayer meeting; nay, He knocks and seeks admittance into your life in the midst of your daily work, your daily struggles, your daily "grind." That is when you need Him most. He is always trying to come into your life, to sup with you. He sees that you need His refreshing presence most of all in the midst of your daily struggles. Listen, therefore, to Jesus as He knocks in the midst of your daily work or rest. Give heed when the Spirit beckons you to look in silent supplication to Him, who follows you day and night.

                                                        O. HALLESBY

The Christian on his knees sees more
than the philosopher on tiptoe.
                    D. L. MOODY

. . . pray to thy Father which is in secret; and thy Father which seeth in secret
shall reward thee openly.
                    Matthew 6:6

How Jesus loved to pray in secret Himself! He had a habit of "rising up a great while before day" and going outdoors—to a mountainside or some other deserted place—to pray. Perhaps because of the small, crowded Palestinian houses, that was the only way He could find privacy and solitude.

Before major decisions—such as His choosing of the twelve apostles—He would pray alone an entire night. And going back to the beginning of His public ministry, we find Jesus going off into the desert for forty days and forty nights of seclusion and concentrated prayer. He knew that power was needed; in secret He would find it.

There are other reasons why Jesus instructs us to pray in secret. Real power in prayer flows only when man's spirit touches God's Spirit. As in worship, so in prayer: "God is a Spirit: and they that worship him must worship him in spirit and in truth" (John 4:24). Secrecy helps us get rid of hindrances to praying with our spirit. For instance, in our room with the door shut, we are not so likely to strut and pose and pretend as we are when another human being is present. We know that we cannot deceive God. Transparent honesty before Him is easier for us in isolation.

CATHERINE MARSHALL
Adventures in Prayer

We are not, therefore, surprised at the amazing power of the Son of man when we find that "in the morning, rising up a great while before day, he went out, and departed into a solitary place, and there prayed" (Mark 1:35). It was while praying that the Holy Spirit descended upon Him. It was only after a whole night of prayer that He selected the twelve apostles from among His disciples. To them He did not unburden His heart concerning His impending death until He had spent time with His Father in prayer. The pressure of business was for Him not the indication for more sleep but for more prayer. In His daily programme the quiet time in a quiet place was as vital as it was precious. See Him even sending the thronging multitude away so that He might go "into a mountain to pray." Does this not speak to us? That the man Christ Jesus should need to pray is probably the greatest indication of all that we also need to pray. He *had* to put aside time for quietness and communion in order to renew those spiritual reserves He needed to live powerfully for God. But not only so, He counted those times alone with His Father as the most precious, joyful and hallowed times of the day.

J. D. C. ANDERSON

An ordinary simple Christian kneels down to say his prayers. He is trying to get in touch with God. But if he is a Christian he knows that what is prompting him to pray is also God: God, so to speak, inside him. But he also knows that all his real knowledge of God comes through Christ, the Man who was God—that Christ is standing beside him, helping him to pray, praying for him.

C. S. LEWIS
Mere Christianity

Lord, when my soul is weary
and my heart is tired and sore,
and I have that failing feeling
that I can't take any more;
then let me know the freshening
found in simple, childlike prayer,
when the kneeling soul knows surely
that a listening Lord is there.

RUTH BELL GRAHAM
Sitting by My Laughing Fire

His prayer life was never at the mercy of moods. Changes of feeling Jesus certainly knew. He was no passionless Stoic. He knew joy and sorrow, smiles and tears, ecstasy and weariness. But through it all, His heart turned to prayer, like the compass to the north. Prayer meant communing with the One He loved best in heaven and earth. Jesus loved God His Father so utterly and so passionately that He could not bear to be away from Him, but used every opportunity the days and nights brought Him to go and speak to the God of His love again. This means that those failures in our own prayer life which we trace back to lack of mood are really, according to Jesus, a symptom of something deeper; they are a symptom of a breakdown of affection. Christ bids us go and give God our love.

JAMES S. STEWART

Our Father which art in heaven, Hallowed be thy name.
Thy kingdom come. Thy will be done in earth, as it is in heaven.
Give us this day our daily bread.
And forgive us our debts, as we forgive our debtors.
And lead us not into temptation, but deliver us from evil:
For thine is the kingdom, and the power, and the glory, for ever. *Amen*.

Matthew 6:9–13

Since we cannot get tomorrow's strength until tomorrow, how futile it is to try today to carry tomorrow's burden! With the burden will come the strength and the guidance. Wasn't this what Jesus meant when He said, "Don't fret about tomorrow. Today's cares are quite enough for today"? And let us not forget that He also said, "I am with you all the days even unto the end."

By all means let us *plan* ahead, but let us live a day at a time, thinking positively, looking with faith and trust at God and committing ourselves wholly to Him Who loves, understands, forgives, accepts and empowers.

> Every day is a fresh beginning;
> Listen, my soul, to the glad refrain,
> And, spite of old sorrow and older sinning,
> And puzzles forecasted, and possible pain,
> Take heart with the day and begin again.

After all, did not Jesus teach us to pray, "Give us *this* day our daily bread"? And day by day He will give us all the other things that we need. No one knows better than He that man does not live by bread alone.

LESLIE D. WEATHERHEAD

> I am the good shepherd, and know my
> sheep, and am known of mine. As the
> Father knoweth me, even so know I the Fa-
> ther: and I lay down my life for the sheep.
> John 10:14, 15

> O Shepherd with the bleeding Feet,
> Good Shepherd with the pleading Voice,
>   What seekest Thou from hill to hill?
> Sweet were the valley pastures, sweet
> The sound of flocks that bleat their joys,
>   And eat and drink at will.
> Is one worth seeking, when Thou hast Thine
>   Ninety and nine?

CHRISTINA G. ROSSETTI

Some years ago travelers noticed the usual sheepfold on a side hill, a low wall built of mud and stones. But they were puzzled to know why, with the opening for the entrance and exit of the sheep, there was no door across it to make the fold safe at night. On being asked the reason for this, the shepherd replied, "I am the door." Further questioning brought out the fact that it was his custom to lie down at night in the opening and then no sheep could get out without his being aware of it. Likewise, no beast or prowler could get at the sheep as they slept, securely guarded by the shepherd in the doorway. Jesus Christ said, "I am the door: by me if any man enter in, he shall be saved and shall go in and out, and find pastures."

JOE MUSSER

Saviour, like a shepherd lead us;
   Much we need Thy tender care;
In Thy pleasant pastures feed us,
   For our use Thy folds prepare.
Blessed Jesus, Blessed Jesus,
   Thou hast bought us, Thine we are;
Blessed Jesus, Blessed Jesus,
   Thou hast bought us, Thine we are.

DOROTHY A. THRUPP

God could have put his message for mankind in flaming letters of lightning across the sky. He could have had it sung by angels for the whole world to hear. Instead, he translated himself into his Son, who walked the hot, dusty roads of Palestine. Today, again, God could translate his message into all the thousand of cultures and languages by running it through some gigantic computer. But he has chosen not to do so. He still chooses to communicate his truth through human personalities. He chooses to walk narrow paths of tropical jungles, hard sidewalks of concrete jungles, and grassy lawns of suburban jungles through translators like you and me, if we will take the risk of letting his treasure be carried to a lost and seeking world in the clay jars of our imperfect lives.

LEIGHTON FORD

Jesus Christ himself is the Way. If we have gone astray from the Way, it is because we have strayed from Jesus Christ. We return to the Way by returning to Jesus Christ. It is not just doctrine about him, or knowledge of him, or experience of the blessings he can give: it is his own living Presence which is the Way.

WESLEY W. NELSON

Jesus Christ will never strong-arm his
way into your life.
                            GRADY B. WILSON

He became what we are that He might
make us what He is.
                            ATHANASIUS

It's a beautiful thing to watch.

God can take a person with all the rough edges and residue from his
days before he knew Jesus and bring about a transformation that is
saintly.

People grow and mature and expand in Jesus and open up as a flower
to the sun, giving a beauty and fragrance that is so very attractive because God does supernatural things in people's lives. "For God is at
work in you, both to will and to work for his good pleasure" (Philippians 2:13 RSV).

It's His pleasure to take someone and do the miraculous. He wills it,
and then He works it.

To see it happen is so indescribably wonderful that there can be no
jealousy about what God is doing.

To see Him work in someone else and bless someone else's life is too
good to want to meddle in.

He may be willing and working for His good pleasure in me, and
that's good, and I'm glad; best of all, I know that you are glad.

But because we are brothers and sisters, I'm happiest as I watch God at
work in you, willing and working to do His good pleasure in you.

And I want to pray, "Lord, make him even happier; do more!"
                            ROGER C. PALMS

Jesus Christ is unique, and one cannot be in His presence and not
reveal the man he really is. Jesus pulls each person from behind his
mask. In the exposure of that bleeding love on the cross, men become
what they really are.

You may think you are wonderful until you stand in the presence of
the One who is purity itself. It is the pure light of God that pierces a
man. You can keep up your pretense of being holy until you stand in
that light. Then immediately there is nowhere to hide, all your masks are
torn away, all your hollow smiles fade.

Revival means to be exposed for what we are. The presence of the Lord
is revealing.
                            FESTO KIVENGERE

When you come to Christ, the Holy Spirit
takes up residence in your heart. Something new is added to your life supernaturally. You are transformed by the renewing
of your mind. A new power, a new dimen-
sion, a new ability to love, a new joy, a new
peace—the Holy Spirit comes in and lives
the Christian life through you.

BILLY GRAHAM

Something beautiful, something good;
All my confusion He understood;
All I had to offer Him was brokenness and strife,
But He made something beautiful of my life.

GLORIA GAITHER

Just as Jesus found it necessary to sweep
the money-changers from the Temple
porch, so we ourselves need a lot of house-
cleaning.

DALE EVANS ROGERS

Dear Master, in whose life I see
All that I would, but fail, to be,
Let Thy clear light forever shine,
To shame and guide this life of mine.

Though what I dream and what I do
In all my days are often two,
Help me, oppressed by things undone,
O Thou whose deeds and dreams were one.

JOHN HUNTER

In 1849 Dostoyevsky, a Russian anarchist, was banished to Siberia.
For four years he was herded with felons in what was known as the
"House of the Dead." But he had with him one book, a New Testament.
This he read over and over, until anger died down in his soul, and he
became a disciple of Christ.

After ten years of banishment, Dostoyevsky returned to his home, to be known thence forward as a philanthropist, a succorer of the helpless and fallen, a teacher of the faith once for all entrusted to the saints. Georg Brandes, by no means sympathetic with the new opinions of the (former) revolutionary, asserts that the sorrow over his death was the grief of the nation, and even Nietzsche acknowledges the reality of his new life in Christ. This great change was wrought solely through the reading of the New Testament.

DAVID M. MC INTYRE

He wakes desires you never may forget;
  He shows you stars you never saw before;
  He makes you share with Him forevermore
The burden of the world's divine regret.

ALFRED TENNYSON

The real Son of God is at your side. He is beginning to turn you into the same kind of thing as Himself. He is beginning, so to speak, to "inject" His kind of life and thought, His Zöe, into you; beginning to turn the tin soldier into a live man. The part of you that does not like it is the part that is still tin.

C. S. LEWIS
Mere Christianity

Live Christ!—and though thy way may be
  In this world's sight adversity,
He who doth heed thy every need
  Shall give thy soul prosperity.

Live Christ!—and though thy path may be
  The narrow street of poverty,
He had not where to lay His Head,
  Yet lived in largest liberty.

Live Christ!—and though thy road may be
  The strait way of humility,
He who first trod that way of God
  Will clothe thee with His dignity.

Live Christ!—and though thy life may be
In much a valedictory,
The heavy cross brings seeming loss,
But wins the crown of victory.

Live Christ!—and all thy life shall be
A High Way of Delivery—
A Royal Road of goodly deeds,
Gold-paved with sweetest charity.

Live Christ!—and all thy life shall be
A sweet uplifting ministry,
A sowing of the fair white seeds
That fruit through all eternity.

JOHN OXENHAM

The melody to "I'd Rather Have Jesus" was written by George Beverly Shea, well-known member of the Billy Graham evangelistic team. As a twenty-two-year-old clerk in a New York insurance firm, he was offered an attractive radio contract. Normally he would have jumped at it, but he was struggling with a call to dedicate his musical talent to God's service. One Sunday, during this decisive time, he arose early to rehearse a hymn he was to sing in church. His eyes fell on a poem placed on the piano by his mother. While reading it, his fingers fell unconsciously to the keyboard and picked out the famous melody to "I'd Rather Have Jesus." And in so doing, the decision was made for his own life.

ROBERT J. HASTINGS

I'd rather have Jesus than silver or gold,
I'd rather be His than have riches untold;
I'd rather have Jesus than houses or lands,
I'd rather be led by His nail-pierced hand.
Than to be the king of a vast domain
Or be held in sin's dread sway;
I'd rather have Jesus than anything
This world affords today.

RHEA F. MILLER

Lay not up for yourselves treasures upon earth, where moth and rust doth corrupt, and where thieves break through and steal:

But lay up for yourselves treasures in heaven, where neither moth nor rust doth corrupt, and where thieves do not break through nor steal:

For where your treasure is, there will your heart be also.

Matthew 6:19–21

Mary is at a lovely social function, at the house of one Simon. There she is, circulating among the friends and guests, but her Lord is all-important to her. "There came unto him a woman." And as a present she brings from her possessions the only treasure she has. It is an alabaster box of ointment, perfectly blended, so that its delightful aroma fills the room. This is what she poured on her Lord. It was the best that she had and she gave him the best.

I am very conscious of the fact that I am personally prone to give the Lord the leftovers in my life; the leftovers of my time, my talent, my day, my week. Not the choicest. Nor the best. Meister Eckhart once said that people would give up to God their possessions, their money, their land, even their children, but they did not want to part with themselves. The self is the treasure. Have you parted with your treasure? Have you given yourself to him in complete commitment?

Christ demands the best in our lives.

MILDRED DIENERT

The blind man, Bartimaeus, threw off his cloak and ran trembling to Jesus. And Jesus said, "What do you want me to do for you?" He said, "Lord, that I may receive my sight." In that moment as he said, "Lord," his spiritual eyes were opened. And Jesus said, "Your faith has made you whole." Notice—not your intellectual understanding, not your money, not your works—but your faith. Faith! That's all it takes! Immediately Bartimaeus, who had been blind all of his life, began to open his eyes, and the first thing he saw was the face of Jesus. What an experience—to open one's eyes and look straight into the strong, tender face of Jesus! Bartimaeus met Jesus and the record says he "followed Jesus in the way." You don't go back to your business, or your home, or your neighborhood, or your friends, or your school, alone. Christ goes with you.

BILLY GRAHAM
Day-by-Day With Billy Graham

Verily, verily, I say unto you, He that
hereth my word, and believeth on him
that sent me, hath everlasting life, and shall
not come into condemnation; but is passed
from death unto life.

John 5:24

As Christ stood on the deck of a storm-tossed little ship, surrounded
by a group of fearful men, calmly He said, "Peace, be still." The winds
and the waves were immediately quiet. Also, the fears of the men were
gone. Not only were their fears of that particular storm conquered, but
also their fears of the future storms. They knew that as long as they had
Christ with them they need not be afraid of a storm.

Long before, the Psalmist learned that same truth. He said, "Yea
though I walk through the valley of the shadow of death." That refers not
just to the experience of death but to any crisis one might be called upon
to face. "I will fear no evil." Why? "For thou art with me."

Now this faith does not mean that every time a storm arises we can call
on God and He will immediately quiet it. Sometimes Christ says to the
winds and the waves, "Peace, be still." But at other times He says it to
the person. Sometimes He changes our situation; at other times He
changes us. Sometimes He removes the mountain from our path; at
other times He enables us to walk over the mountains.

CHARLES L. ALLEN

My most cherished possession I wish I
could leave you is my faith in Jesus Christ,
for with Him and nothing else you can be
happy, but without Him and with all else
you'll never be happy.

PATRICK HENRY

To believe is to commit . . . . In particular belief I commit myself
spiritually to Jesus Christ, and determine in that thing to be dominated
by the Lord alone. When I stand face to face with Jesus Christ and he
says to me, "Believest thou this?" I find that faith is as natural as breathing, and I am staggered that I was so stupid as not to trust him before.

OSWALD CHAMBERS

Jesus said unto him, If thou canst believe, all things are possible to him that believeth. And straightway the father of the child cried out, and said with tears, Lord, I believe; help thou mine unbelief.

Mark 9:23, 24

What a glorious promise: "All things are possible to him that believeth"! And yet it is just the greatness of the promise that constitutes the trial of faith. At first we do not really believe its truth. But when we have grasped it, then comes the real trial in the thought: Such a wonder-working faith is utterly beyond my reach.

But what constitutes the trial of faith soon becomes its triumph. How can this be? When Christ said to the father of the child, "If thou canst believe, all things are possible to him that believeth," he felt that this was only casting him into deeper despair. How could his faith be able to work the miracle? But as he looked into the face of Christ, and the love of the tender eye touched his heart, he felt sure that this blessed Man not only had the power to heal his child, but the power too to inspire him with the needed faith. The impression Christ produced upon him made not only the one miracle of the healing possible, but the second miracle too that he should have so great a faith. And with tears he cried, "Lord, I believe; help Thou mine unbelief." The very greatness of faith's trial was the greatness of faith's triumph.

ANDREW MURRAY

Give me faith, Lord, and let me help others to find it.

LEO TOLSTOY

Open all the doors and windows of your soul to the Lord. Don't keep any rooms locked or closed off to him. Let Jesus take over. The depth of the faith that releases the power of God is measured by your willingness to let God direct your life. Raise yourself up to him as a gift. Surrender your life and your heart to him.

JOHN POWELL

All the way my Saviour leads me—
    What have I to ask beside?
Can I doubt His tender mercy,
    Who through life has been my guide?

Heavenly peace, divinest comfort,
    Here by faith in Him to dwell!
For I know, whate'er befall me,
    Jesus doeth all things well.

FANNY J. CROSBY

I frankly believe that about 98 percent of all the guidance that you and I need is contained in the Bible. I believe that if we understand the Bible, we will see Jesus. I believe that if we understand the Bible, we will see the way of God. Almost every decision that comes to us will be guided by Scripture, if we have Scripture hidden in our hearts.

Thy word have I hid in mine heart, that I might not sin against thee.

Psalms 119:11

PAT ROBERTSON

Blessed are the poor in spirit: for theirs is the kingdom of heaven.

Matthew 5:3

Poor . . . I can't imagine anyone *wanting* to be poor . . . to be totally destitute, in need, anxious, hopeless, frightened . . . . Surely our loving Lord doesn't want this for us?

And yet, Jesus says that only if we are poor will we be happy . . . . "Blessed are the poor in spirit: for theirs is the kingdom of heaven."

There were many poor people sitting at Jesus' feet when He spoke these words, and He wasn't telling them that they never had it so good. No—Jesus had great compassion for human need, and the sight of the suffering poor grieved Him. Obviously He was talking about something beyond physical need.

All right . . . suppose I were in the crowd that came to hear Him speak—and suppose I were poor . . . I wouldn't have come to get food—He had none. I wouldn't have come for money—He had none. But perhaps I would have come because I needed something else, something that only Jesus could give me.

Yes—now there seems to be new meaning in the word *poor*. I was thinking of it in terms of the kind of poverty we're trying to eliminate from our world . . . starvation, disease, ignorance. But there is another kind of poverty—one that is much worse and not as visible. There is a poverty of the spirit. And that's what Jesus is talking about in the first Beatitude.

"Blessed are the poor in spirit . . . ." This seems to be the center from which the other Beatitudes radiate. For unless we know how poor we are without Christ, we'll never reach out for Him. If we feel we can take care of ourselves, why ask for help—even from God?

Come to think of it, the happiest people I know are those who have tried and failed—even hit bottom—and then reached out for help. Realizing their spiritual bankruptcy, they asked Jesus to take over their lives. They entered the kingdom through the door of their own need, and they were met by God's grace.

COLLEEN TOWNSEND EVANS
A New Joy

Christ is rich, who will maintain you: He is a king, who will provide you: He is a sumptuous entertainer, who will feast you: He is beautiful, who will give in abundance all that can make you happy.

EDMUND CAMPION

Our Lord opened the understanding of his disciples. He sought entrance for truth by that avenue. He does so still.

T. C. HAMMOND

. . . All power is given unto me in heaven and in earth.

Matthew 28:18

Before Christ gave His disciples their Great Commission to begin that great world conquest which should aim at bringing His Gospel to every creature, He first revealed Himself in His divine power as a partner with

God Himself, the Almighty One. It was the faith of this that enabled the
disciples to undertake the work in all simplicity and boldness. They had
begun to know Him in that mighty resurrection power which had conquered sin and death; there was nothing too great for Him to command
or for them to undertake.

Every disciple of Jesus Christ who desires to take part in the victory
that overcometh the world needs time, and faith, and the Holy Spirit, to
come under the full conviction that it is as the servant of the omnipotent
Lord Jesus that he is to take his part in the work. He is to count literally
upon the daily experience of being "strong in the Lord and in the power
of His might." The word of promise gives the courage to obey implicitly
the word of command.

ANDREW MURRAY

With His power,
    He would like to accomplish
    great things through me,
    using me
    to mold others by my influence,
    to change the direction
    of the coastline in some lives,
    to shape surroundings for Him—
    gently or firmly,
    to lift great logs of guilt
    or worry
    from shoulders,
    to make safe caves for those who need
    comfort from storms.
All this, He would do through His power in me in
    my every day walk.

PAMELA REEVE

"If anyone loves me he will keep my word,
and my Father will love him,
and we shall come to him
and make our home with him.
Those who do not love me do not keep my words.
And my word is not my own:
it is the word of the one who sent me.

I have said these things to you
while still with you;
but the Advocate, the Holy Spirit,
whom the Father will send in my name,
will teach you everything
and remind you of all I have said to you.
Peace I bequeath to you,
my own peace I give you,
a peace the world cannot give, this is my gift to you.
Do not let your hearts be troubled or afraid.
You heard me say:
I am going away, and shall return.
If you loved me you would have been glad to know that I am
    going to the Father,
for the Father is greater than I."

John 14:24–28 JB

Death is not beautiful. It separates soul from body, husband from wife, father from children; and Jesus let it be known that death is not beautiful when He stood at Lazarus's grave and wept.

Jesus wept not just with sympathy, not just with sorrow for Lazarus's sisters and friends, but also with anger at the enemy—death. Satan brought death with his taunting temptation to Eve and Adam to choose to believe him rather than God's warning. Jesus wept with a strong emotion, not with polite tears as if to enter an "atmosphere of mourning." His tears were real, and the strength of emotion behind them was real. The amazing thing to me is that Jesus wept *after* He had already said to Martha, "I am the resurrection and the life: he that believeth in me, though he were dead, yet shall he live: And whosoever liveth and believeth in me shall never die. Believest thou this?" (John 11:25, 26). He believed completely what He had said, yet He wept.

Jesus was speaking of the *reality* of the resurrection of bodies which will be changed bodies—just as He Himself would later demonstrate with His own resurrected body—as well as speaking of the fact that He had the power to raise Lazarus.

EDITH SCHAEFFER

Now our LORD Jesus Christ himself, and
God, even our Father, which hath loved us,
and hath given us everlasting consolation
and good hope through grace.

2 Thessalonians 2:16

To me, what Jesus did at the tomb of Lazarus sets the world on fire; it becomes a great shout into the morass of the twentieth century. Jesus came to the tomb of Lazarus. The One who claims to be God stood before the tomb, and the Greek language makes it very plain that he had two emotions. The first was tears for Lazarus; but the second emotion was blinding anger. He was furious; and he could be furious at the evil of death without being furious with himself as God. This is tremendous in the context of the twentieth century. When I look at evil—the abnormal cruelty which is not the thing as God made it—my reaction should be the same. I am able not only to cry for the evil, but I can be angry at the evil—as long as I am careful that egoism does not enter into my reaction. I have a basis to fight the thing which is abnormal to what God has made.

FRANCIS A. SCHAEFFER

MARTHA'S AWAKENING

"Dear Lord," she cried silently to herself as her eyes found Jesus in the crowd. "You are not just my friend—you are my Saviour, my Redeemer, my Lord. You are God come down in flesh to me, to my brother, sister, friends—no, even to the whole world. How could I have been so close to you, yet almost missed you?

"You were here with me in my house and in my village, but I was always outside your love rushing wildly about.

"You were here within me, but I was not with you. You called me, but my ears were stopped, and I was deaf to your pleadings.

"I did not sit at your feet with Mary, because I would not stop my serving long enough to listen to you.

"But today, here at the tomb, you have broken past my deafness; you have bathed me in your forgiveness; you have wrapped me in your splendor; you have taken the blindness from my eyes.

"I do not know why I came to love you so late, my Lord. But I do love you, and I know who you are now, Jesus of Nazareth. You are my God, my King, my Saviour, my Messiah."

The wonder and depth of her words overwhelmed her. Martha uttered a small cry out loud, and with new understanding thought to herself, *Oh, Lord, that is why you sent the message that Lazarus's sickness would not end in death, but in giving glory to God. Here, today, in your prayer you said you were doing this so that the people gathered here would believe.*

Lord, did you know I would be one of those believers? Did you know what today would be for me? Martha looked at Jesus, and she knew he had heard all her thoughts, for he raised his head, nodded silently to her, and his smile was filled with warm compassion and total understanding.

JOYCE LANDORF

Before He left His disciples, Christ promised that He would send a Comforter to help them in the trials, cares, and temptations of life. This word comforter means "one that helps alongside." He is the Holy Spirit, the powerful Third Person of the Trinity. The moment you are born again, He takes up residence in your heart. You may not emotionally feel Him there, but here you must exercise faith. Believe it! Accept it as a fact of faith! He is in your heart to help you. We are told that He sheds the love of God abroad in our hearts. He produces the fruit of the spirit: "love, joy, peace, long-suffering, gentleness, goodness, faith, meekness, temperance." We cannot possibly manufacture this fruit in our own strength. It is supernaturally manufactured by the Holy Spirit who lives in our hearts!

BILLY GRAHAM
Day-by-Day With Billy Graham

If I go away, the Comforter will come unto you. He shall glorify Me; for He shall take of Mine, and shall declare it unto you.

See John 16:7, 14

"And they were on the road, going up to Jerusalem, and Jesus was walking ahead of them; and they were amazed, and those who followed were afraid." He's out ahead of us now, beckoning us on to our Jerusalem. Here is reality—life as it is. Here are the people and problems we submerged, sublimated, struggled to forget. We feel like the disciples, amazed at his determination and afraid at what might happen. But, with him in his Jerusalem and ours, we are about to learn the dynamics of a love that never gives up.

Jesus went to Jerusalem because it was God's will for him. It was the reason he was born. He knew that it would mean the cross: "Behold, we are going up to Jerusalem; and the Son of man will be delivered to the chief priests and the scribes, and they will condemn him to death, and deliver him to the Gentiles, and they will mock him and spit upon him and scourge him, and kill him; and after three days he will rise.''

Jesus' commitment to Jerusalem was based on two absolutely necessary elements of a love that never gives up. He was convinced that it was God's will for him to go and he knew that his death would be superseded by the resurrection. The worst that man would do to him would be superseded by the best that God could do. Those two ingredients must also be the basis of our commitment. Don't go into your Jerusalem until it is God's undeniable will for you! But when it is his time to face reality, face it knowing that he will validate your commitment with his victory.

LLOYD J. OGILVIE
Life Without Limits

EVIL DAYS

When He came into Jerusalem
In the week before the feast,
He was hailed by crowds with palms
And hosannas to His glory.

But days grew frightful, grim,
Men's eyebrows knit with scorn,
Their hearts unmoved by love.
And soon came the evil end.

The heavens lay heavy as lead,
Crushing the blocks of houses.
The Pharisees came for proof,
And wheedled like sly old foxes.

He was thrown to the city scum
By powers supporting the Temple.
With the selfsame zeal they had praised
His name, they cursed Him at last.

The rabble from every square
Gathered to peer in the gateways;
They jostled forward and backwards
And waited for the end to come.

The alleys whispered their tales
And the squares their secret talk.
He remembered the flight to Egypt
And His childhood as if in a dream.

He remembered the silent desert,
The majestic mountain top
Where Satan had tempted Him
With kingdoms in all the world.

And the marriage feast at Cana,
And the guests who gazed in awe,
And the sea whereon He had walked
To the boat as across dry land.

And the poor who met in a hovel,
His descent to the vault with a light—
How the candle died down in fear
When Lazarus rose from the dead.

BORIS PASTERNAK

The teaching I gave you
was given me personally by the Lord himself,
and it was this:
        the Lord Jesus,
in the same night in which he was betrayed,
        took bread and when he had given thanks
        he broke it and said,
"This is my body—and it is for you.
Do this in remembrance of me."
        Similarly, when supper was ended,
        he took the cup saying,
"This cup is the new agreement made by my blood:
    do this, whenever you drink it,
    in remembrance of me."
This can only mean that whenever you eat this bread and drink this cup,
    you are proclaiming the Lord's death until he comes again.
So that, whoever eats the bread or drinks the cup of the Lord
    without proper reverence
    is sinning against the body and blood of the Lord.

No, a man should thoroughly examine himself,
and only then
should he eat the bread or drink of the cup.
He that eats and drinks carelessly
is eating and drinking a condemnation of himself,
for he is blind to the presence of the Body.

1 Corinthians 11:23–29 PHILLIPS

In the holy sacrament of the altar there are three things we must observe: the sign, which should be outward, visible, and in a bodily shape; the thing signified, which is inward, spiritual, and in the mind of man; and faith, which makes use of both . . . . There is no closer, deeper or more indivisible union than that which takes place between the food and the body which the food nourishes. Christ is so united to us in the sacrament [of the Lord's Supper] that He acts as if He were ourselves. Our sins assail Him; His righteousness defends us.

MARTIN LUTHER

The Lord's Supper testifies to us that we have complete forgiveness of all our sins through the one sacrifice of Jesus Christ which He Himself has accomplished on the Cross once for all.

The Heidelberg Catechism

The body of Jesus was broken for us, crucified, dead, buried and risen, that we might be one bread and one body with him, broken by repentance, crucified by faith, dead unto sin, buried and raised to newness of life in him.

NORMAN P. GRUBB

Break Thou the bread of life,
Dear Lord, to me,
As Thou didst break the loaves
Beside the sea;
Beyond the sacred page
I seek Thee, Lord;
My spirit pants for Thee,
O Living Word!

Bless Thou the truth, dear Lord,
  To me, to me,
As Thou didst bless the bread
  By Galilee;
Then shall all bondage cease,
  All fetters fall;
And I shall find my peace,
  My All in All.

MARY A. LATHBURY

When we come to Christ's table to commune, we come with a prayer that we may be filled with the fulness of his life, may grow into his likeness, and may evermore dwell in him and he in us.

HOWARD W. ELLIS

He was the Word that spake it,
  He took the bread and brake it;
And what that Word did make it,
  I do believe and take it.

JOHN DONNE

All those who journey, soon or late,
Must pass within the garden's gate;
Must kneel alone in darkness there,
And battle with some fierce despair.
God pity those who cannot say:
"Not mine but thine"; who only pray:
"Let this cup pass," and cannot see
The purpose in Gethsemane.

ELLA WHEELER WILCOX

. . . "My Father, if it be possible, let this cup pass from me; nevertheless, not as I will, but as thou wilt."

Matthew 26:39 RSV

No one wants to die—that is—no one in his right mind; even Jesus Christ did not want to die. Even though he sensed that his death was the will of his Father for the redemption of the world, he was not leaping to the Crucifixion. He told his disciples, with a heavy heart, "My soul is very sorrowful, even to death; remain here, and watch with me" (*see* Matthew 26:38). The pain of impending death filled his whole being with a deep desire for companionship; he did not want to be alone, although he knew the cross was to be a lonely experience. "Come watch with me"—or to paraphrase, "Stay awake with me, don't go to sleep on me, because I need you"—was a cry coming from the depths of a very real man. Jesus did not want to die.

And yet, something of greater motivation came through. ". . . nevertheless not my will, but thine, be done" (Luke 22:42 RSV). Accountability! It ruled the life of our Lord! He considered nothing more important than the will of his Father. He had been sent by the Father (and how many times he reminds us of that), and he was to do the will of the One who sent him. That was the long and the short of it. He was accountable to God, and he did not count that accountability as detrimental to his personality or his freedom. He was free to carry out his Father's will.

Following the example of his Lord, the Apostle Paul considered himself a debtor to all men, accountable to the nations that knew nothing of Christ. And to those who believed, he felt he was a servant for their benefit. "I am hard pressed between the two. My desire is to depart and be with Christ, for that is far better. But to remain in the flesh is more necessary on your account. Convinced of this, I know that I shall remain and continue with you all, for your progress and joy in the faith" (Philippians 1:23–25 RSV).

The theme is simple and powerful: What happens to me matters to you, and I hold myself accountable to my brothers and sisters in the covenant of Christ. To deny this fact is to step out into the desert of isolation and loneliness.

LOUIS H. EVANS, JR.

Christ was wonderful in the life he lived on earth. Everything that yielded to him participated in wonder. It was just another wedding until Jesus arrived, and he transformed it into an occasion that is still pondered by devout souls. Ordinary servants put ordinary water into ordinary stone pots and then—the extraordinary happened! The wonder of it all—water was turned into wine! But this is the wonder of his life; whatever he touched took on new substance and new meaning. Peter and his fisherman friends would have lived ordinary lives, and died ordinary deaths, had they never met Jesus. Peter had caught fish before he met Jesus; but when Jesus was giving the orders, catching fish was a totally new experience. "Launch out into the deep!" "Cast the net on the right side of the ship!" And Peter had experienced storms on the Sea of Galilee, but the experience was different when Jesus Christ was in control. "Peace! Be still!" Jesus even let Peter walk on the water!

Whatever Jesus touched, he blessed and beautified and made wonderful. He tried to open men's eyes to see the world around them: the splendor of the lilies, the freedom of the sparrows, the miracle of the children. He took everyday bread and wine and gave these necessities a depth of meaning that transformed them into luxuries of God's grace. A little seed suddenly becomes a sermon: "The seed is the Word of God." Water is a picture of the Holy Spirit. A lost sheep is a lost soul. He wrote in the dust and confounded the angry religious leaders. Perhaps the greatest wonder of all, he transformed a shameful cross into the meeting place of God's love and man's sin.

WARREN W. WIERSBE

Lord Jesus, Your life here on earth brought comfort to the brokenhearted—hope to those who had never known what it was to have Someone love them. You healed the sick in mind and body. As we read of Your life through the Bible, may we give ourselves unreservedly to You, that through Your Holy Spirit, we may continue to bring Your comfort and love to our neighbors. Dear Lord—they are Your sheep for whom You suffered. Thank You, beloved Jesus. Amen.

—J. W. B.

Jesus—His Cross

Our Promise of Life Forever

But His lone Cross and crown of thorns
Endure when crowns and empires fall.
The might of His undying Love
In dying conquered all.

JOHN OXENHAM

As the days approached that first Good Friday, Jesus suffered indescribable agony. In the Garden of Gethsemane He wrestled in prayer to God—"Father, if thou be willing, remove this cup from me: nevertheless not my will, but thine, be done" (Luke 22:42). The Scripture continues: "And being in an agony he prayed more earnestly: and his sweat was as it were great drops of blood falling down to the ground" (v. 44).

Jesus knew the suffering He would have to face upon that Cross—He knew He would have to endure the reviling, the cruel taunts of the mob, the unbelievable suffering at the hands of the soldiers. He also knew that this was why He had come into the world—that there was no one else who could pay the price of our sin and, in one of the greatest acts of humility, He willingly went to such a shameful death for you and me.

Betrayed by His disciple, Judas of Iscariot, He suffered humiliation at the hands of His judges and the soldiers. Beaten unmercifully—mocked at, a crown of thorns jammed into His beloved head—He never once opened His mouth to protest.

As Jesus dragged the Cross through the streets of Jerusalem, He was also weighed down with the sin of the world. As the suffering, beaten, exhausted Jesus stumbled and sank beneath the weight of the Cross, a man standing in the crowd watched—only in curiosity. He never dreamed that he would be called upon to perform one of the last acts of kindness to the Man who was his Saviour.

Perhaps his first reaction was one of resentment, when the soldiers singled out Simon of Cyrene to perform the menial task of carrying Jesus' Cross. Little did he know that this act would change his whole life. We read of other acts of kindness—Mary washing Jesus' feet, Martha serving Him meals—but Simon carried the Cross of the Redeemer of the world!

Later, this man was to accept Christ and have his whole life changed and his two sons, Alexander and Rufus, would grow to be prominent figures in the Church.

Today it is fashionable to wear jewelry in the form of a cross, whether you believe in Jesus or not. At the time of Jesus' Crucifixion it would have been the same as if we wore a miniature of an electric chair or a gibbet around our necks. The Cross is taken many times for granted—just another adornment. But for our Lord it meant the cruelest of all deaths.

In our own lives when we come to the Cross, we stand amazed at the love of this Saviour. We must never cease to be amazed that the Son of God would bear our sins upon His body, on that cruel instrument of torture. To the repentant thief, writhing on the cross beside Him, He said, ". . . Today shalt thou be with me in paradise" (Luke 23:43). In spite of His own agony, He still had time to care for this man's need and because of Him we too are promised life forever. Not because of *our* righteous lives but because of His!

Jesus chose to die on Calvary and in that magnificent, heroic, sacrificial death, He fulfilled the prophecy written hundreds of years before in Isaiah:

He is despised and rejected of men; a man of sorrows, and acquainted with grief: and we hid as it were our faces from him; he was despised, and we esteemed him not.

Surely he hath borne our griefs, and carried our sorrows: yet we did esteem him stricken, smitten of God, and afflicted.

But he was wounded for our transgressions, he was bruised for our iniquities: the chastisement of our peace was upon him; and with his stripes we are healed.

All we like sheep have gone astray; we have turned every one to his own way; and the Lord hath laid on him the iniquity of us all.

He was oppressed, and he was afflicted, yet he opened not his mouth: he is brought as a lamb to the slaughter, and as a sheep before her shearers is dumb, so he openeth not his mouth.

He was taken from prison and from judgment: and who shall declare his generation? for he was cut off out of the land of the living: for the transgression of my people was he stricken . . . .

He shall see of the travail of his soul, and shall be satisfied: by his knowledge shall my righteous servant justify many; for he shall bear their iniquities.

Isaiah 53:3–8; 53:11

—*J. W. B.*

When I survey the wondrous cross
  On which the Prince of Glory died,
My richest gain I count but loss,
  And pour contempt on all my pride.

Forbid it, Lord, that I should boast,
  Save in the death of Christ, my God;
All the vain things that charm me most,
  I sacrifice them to His blood.

See, from His head, His hands, His feet,
  Sorrow and love flow mingled down;
Did e'er such love and sorrow meet,
  Or thorns compose so rich a crown?

Were the whole realm of nature mine,
  That were a present far too small;
Love so amazing, so divine,
  Demands my soul, my life, my all. *Amen.*

ISAAC WATTS

I, if I be lifted up from the earth, will
draw all men unto me. This he said, sig-
nifying what death he should die.

John 12:32, 33

When all is over, and the Prisoner has been marched away to Golgotha, it is not He who has been judged by them: it is they who have
been judged by Him. Face to face each of them—Caiaphas, Pilate,
Herod—stood with the Son of man for a brief hour, and His searchlight
played upon their souls, revealing their inmost nature, and showing
them up for all the world and for all time to see. On that dark, crowded
night, the real Judge was Christ. And where Caiaphas, Pilate and Herod
stood that night, every soul at some stage of its life-journey must
stand—face to face with Jesus, in the place of decision: and each soul's
verdict on the Lord of all good life is, in a deep and solemn sense,
Christ's verdict on itself.

JAMES S. STEWART

And when they were come to the place,
which is called Calvary, there they crucified
him, and the malefactors, one on the right
hand, and the other on the left.

Luke 23:33

There is a green hill far away,
  Outside a city wall,
Where the dear Lord was crucified,
  Who died to save us all.

We may not know, we cannot tell
  What pains He had to bear,
But we believe it was for us
  He hung and suffered there.

Oh, dearly, dearly He has loved,
  And we must love Him too,
And trust in His redeeming blood,
  And try His works to do.

He died that we might be forgiven,
  He died to make us good,
That we might go at last to heaven,
  Saved by His precious blood.

There was no other good enough
  To pay the price of sin;
He only could unlock the gate
  Of heaven and let us in.

CECIL FRANCES ALEXANDER

There are some who would have Christ
cheap. They would have Him without the
Cross. But the price will not come down.

SAMUEL RUTHERFORD

It was high noon as workmen arranged the crosses on the ground.
  The three condemned prisoners stood together—Dysmas and Gestas
and Jesus, while the soldiers shoved back the crowd and the common
workmen disposed the crosses on the ground near the holes and heaps
of fresh earth.

High noon, and the sun brightly shining on bay trees and laurel over yonder,but on the four edges of the world clouds were gathering. In spring is it not unusual for clouds to begin gathering on the four horizons all at once? Few noticed the dark ring around the lower part of the sky. They had other things to look at: the three cross-trees laid out now and ladders being bolted and braced, and men with hammers and spikes and other men with spears goading each prisoner to lie down on his cross.

It was a quick business; the three victims were tired out, inert, incapable of resistance. They stretched Jesus out on the prostrate device, fingers in His armpits and palms forcing down His thighs and holding His head in the middle of the crosspiece, and they held Him so while they hammered huge pointed spikes through His palms—then nailed His feet to the main piece. Up now, hoist high, and dump the foot of the cross in the open hole.

So, there, and at last, the will of Annas and Caiphas was fully done. Jesus was crucified between two thieves, the three gaunt crosses with their suffering human beings uplifted upon them making sharp, bleak silhouettes against the paling sky.

One would have thought, then, that with this finality malice would wither, but it was not like that.

At mocking Pilate's orders—strange commands of a strange man who meant the priests to be confronted with a reminder—a sign nailed up on the cross over the head of Jesus, an inscription in three languages: Latin, Greek, and Aramaic:

"Jesus of Nazareth, the King of the Jews!"

FULTON OURSLER

But we see Jesus, who for a little while was made lower than the angels, crowned with glory and honor because of the suffering of death, so that by the grace of God he might taste death for every one.

Hebrews 2:9 RSV

THE OFFENCE OF THE CROSS

It may be well to remind ourselves of what death by crucifixion meant in the thoughts of the ancient world. With the passing of the years, Christendom has cast a halo of beauty round the cross. We build our churches in the shape of a cross. We emblazon the cross on the flags of the nations. Beneath the cross we bury our dear dead. We take a Red Cross, and with it symbolise the ministry of healing. Our poets and hymn-writers sing to us of "the wondrous cross," "the blessed cross." But all this ought not to hide from us the fact that originally the cross was a thing unspeakably shameful and degrading. "Cursed is everyone that hangeth on a tree," said Paul, quoting Deuteronomy 23. That was how Jewish feeling expressed it; and Roman sentiment was the same. "This cruellest, most hideous of punishments," said Cicero, using words in which you can almost hear the shudder—"crudelissimum taeterrimum-que supplicium." "Never may it," he said elsewhere, "come near the bodies of Roman citizens, never near their thoughts or eyes or ears!" Devised in the first instance in semi-barbaric Oriental lands, death by crucifixion was reserved by the Romans for slaves and for criminals of the most abandoned kind. It was a fate of utter ignominy. It was the hangman's rope of the ancient world. Small wonder that when the first Apostles began their world-mission, they found one prejudice everywhere confronting them, among Jews and Gentiles alike—"the offence, the stumbling-block, of the cross" (Galatians 5:11; 1 Corinthians 1:23). That the Messiah should die was hard enough to credit; but that He should die such a death was utterly beyond belief. Yet so it was. Everything which Christ ever touched—the cross included—He adorned and transfigured and haloed with splendour and beauty; but let us never forget out of what appalling depths He has set the cross on high.

JAMES S. STEWART

No pain, no palm; no thorns, no throne;
no gall, no glory; no cross, no crown.

WILLIAM PENN

THE CENTURION

If you try to visualise the scene that first Good Friday morning, you can't miss the soldiers. They escorted the prisoners along the road to Calvary; on that skull-shaped hill they were the execution-squad. The centurion in charge of them had picked out Simon of Cyrene from the crowd and ordered him to carry the cross for Jesus. He gave the orders, he stood by, he saw what happened. However hardened he may have been to this kind of thing, he was on duty throughout. And that's all we know about him; that, and the fact that he made a very odd remark when he saw that Jesus was dead.

A Roman centurion; a sort of non-commissioned officer, like a sergeant-major. And the Romans had some well-seasoned jokes about their centurions, too. But have you noticed what a very good show Roman centurions put up in the New Testament? Remember, they were officers in a foreign army of occupation. Those we meet seem to have been of a type—intelligent, reliable, sympathetic. The only other picked out for special mention is this one. We don't even know his name. There's a legend that it was Longinus, but that may have been only a nickname—like "Lofty, the Sergeant-Major."

But we know he had plenty of opportunity for watching Jesus very closely; he'd had charge of Him ever since the trial by Pilate ended; he saw and heard all that happened on Calvary; he listened to that amazing prayer, even as the nails were driven into Our Lord's hands and feet: "Father, forgive them, for they know not what they do!" Then, through slow hours of anguish, he watched and waited for the end; heard the Saviour's words as He hung and suffered there—heard the great shout of triumph at the end: "It is finished." And all the time, an impression was being built up in his mind; at last, almost in spite of himself, he had to say: "Truly, this man was a Son of God!" It was the heart-felt tribute of a rough soldier, who said about the finest thing he could say about Jesus.

A. E. GOULD

GAMBLER

And sitting down, they watched Him there,
The soldiers did;
There, while they played with dice,
He made His sacrifice,
And died upon the Cross to rid
God's world of sin.

He was a gambler, too, my Christ,
He took His life and threw
It for a world redeemed.
And ere His agony was done,
Before the westering sun went down,
Crowning that day with crimson crown,
He knew that He had won.

G. A. STUDDERT-KENNEDY

CHRIST ON TRIAL

When Jesus was on trial, they did not go and summon His friends—those who knew Him best. They did not go and bring up Zacchaeus of Jericho; they did not bring up that poor man that had the legion of devils cast out of him; they did not bring the blind man of Jericho—they brought His enemies. Let Caiaphas tell his own story—suppose he stood in my place. Caiaphas, just tell us what was the evidence you found against Jesus. "I said to Him I adjure Thee by the living God, art Thou the Son of God? And He said 'I am.' When I heard it I tore my mantle and said He was guilty of blasphemy." That is what we glory in, His being the Son of God. Stephen said, when the curtains were lifted, and he caught a glimpse of glory. "I see Jesus standing at the right hand of God." The testimony is perfectly overwhelming that Jesus Christ was the Son of God as well as the Son of David. Even the devils called him "that Son of the Most High God."

DWIGHT L. MOODY

It was while the soldiers were throwing the dice that Jesus looked down and saw that He was not alone. Moving slowly forward through the crowd, coming ever closer to the cross, were three women—three Marys close at hand. Mary, His mother, stood at the foot of the cross. And Mary, the wife of Cleophas, His mother's sister, knelt beside her; Mary of Magdalen, out of whom he had cast seven devils, was prostrate on the earth.

And who standing beside His blessed mother? John! Yes, it was John! John, the well-beloved disciple. This was why you hovered on the far outside of the crowd; you were waiting to bring Mother here.

With a sudden access of strength Jesus called out in the premature gloaming that was creeping in:

"Woman, behold your son!"

With infinite tenderness He called to her; and then, turning to John, the drops of sweat glistening on His neck and forehead and cheeks, He summed up all the concern and compassion in His heart in these words to His dear follower:

"Behold your mother!" And from that day on John would be like another son to Mary. But his devotion was a symbol of a greater service, for Jesus had spoken to mankind, had showed all living the symbol of motherhood.

FULTON OURSLER

A CENTURION SPEAKS TO MARY, THE MOTHER OF JESUS:

I tell you, woman, this dead son of yours, disfigured, shamed, spat upon, has built a kingdom this day that can never die. The living glory of him rules it. The earth is his and he made it. He and his brothers have been moulding and making it through the long ages. They are the only ones who ever really did possess it; not the proud, not the idle, not the wealthy, not the vaunting empires of the world. Something has happened up here on this hill today to shake all our kingdoms of blood and fear to the dust. The earth is his, the earth is theirs, and they made it. The meek, the terrible meek, the fierce agonizing meek, are about to enter their inheritance.

CHARLES RANN KENNEDY

GOOD FRIDAY

Am I a stone, and not a sheep,
   That I can stand, O Christ, beneath Thy cross,
   To number drop by drop Thy Blood's slow loss,
And yet not weep?

Not so those women loved
   Who with exceeding grief lamented Thee;
   Not so fallen Peter weeping bitterly;
Not so the thief was moved;

Not so the Sun and Moon
   Which hid their faces in a starless sky.
   A horror of great darkness at broad noon—
I, only I.

Yet give not o'er
   But seek Thy sheep, true Shepherd of the flock;
   Greater than Moses, turn and look once more
And smite a rock.

CHRISTINA G. ROSSETTI

Last words are precious words; how we cling to them, and let them gently stir through the memory and persist through the years. Men build about them great paeans and songs.

The last words of Jesus, matchless for pathos and forgiveness and trust, form a garland of seven flowers that shall never fade while the world lasts. There are three before the darkness; one during the darkness, and three after the darkness. The first is the word of intercession: "Father, forgive them, they know not what they do." These hired soldiers, who are driving the nails and raising the cross, He would forgive them.

The second word is the world of hope beyond death, spoken to the young thief: "This day shalt thou be with me in paradise." The third word is one of loving provision, "Woman, behold thy son." One of the tenderest acts in all history. Jesus did not forget His mother; He was a son as well as a Saviour; a Son to the last. The fourth: "Why hast thou forsaken me?" spoken in the awful darkness, we shall never understand. It is the word of loneliness. The first three were spoken for others: He cared for others before He thought of Himself. The great heart broke and He cried, "My God." He lost His sense of God for a moment but not His trust. As the darkness passes He speaks three more words—"I thirst!" "It is finished," the word of victory. The seventh word is the word of trust—"Father, into thy hands." "Father!" a precious word for God. The word of supreme confidence, of assurance, of victory.

A. E. GREGORY

"Into thy hands." This final word of Jesus brings completion of faith for others, completion of faith for us. Faith in Him leads us at last to trust. We yield our all to Him because we believe what He said about God and life as true.

JAMES W. KENNEDY

HIS HANDS

The hands of Christ
    Seem very frail,
For they were broken
    By a nail.

But only they reach
    Heaven at last
Whom these frail, broken
    Hands hold fast.

JOHN RICHARD MORELAND

THE CROSS STANDS

God forbid that I should glory, save in the cross of our Lord Jesus Christ, by whom the world is crucified unto me; and I unto the world (Galatians 6:14). The preaching of the cross is to them that perish foolishness; but unto us which are saved it is the power of God (1 Corinthians 1:18).

The author of the hymn "In the Cross of Christ I Glory" was Sir John Bowring. The early Portuguese colonists built at Macao, China, on the crest of a hill on the south coast, a massive cathedral with a splendid approach of stone steps. A violent typhoon nearly wrecked the building; only the front wall remained intact. On the summit of the facade stands a great bronze cross, defying storm and weather. When Sir John Bowring, then governor of Hong Kong, visited Macao in 1825, he was much impressed by that uplifted cross which seemed to defy the ravages of time and storm. The sight inspired him to write the poem:

> In the Cross of Christ I glory,
> Tow'ring o'er the wrecks of time;
> And the light of sacred story
> Gathers round its head sublime.

Since that day thousands of visitors have looked upon that same ruin and cross. Some look with indifference, some with curiosity, some with reverence, but few have known that the hymn sung so long by the Church around the world was written by the British governor of Hong Kong as he beheld that same cross which stands today.

KEITH L. BROOKS

The work of the Lord Jesus . . . is represented by "the blood" shed for our justification through "the remission of sins." The blood deals with what we have done, whereas the cross deals with what we are. The blood disposes of our sins, while the cross strikes at the root of our capacity for sin.

WATCHMAN NEE

Oh, precious death!
There was no glory there.
The powers of hell
Tearing across His body
Echoing through a soul left empty
Poured out
Crying out
Hanging His head
Deserted
Alone as only God could stand
To be alone . . .
And all for me.
Blood-drops there translated
The love of God
To words that I could hear
And understand.

                        MARGARET GABEL

Christ takes it for granted that men are bad. Until we really feel this assumption of His to be true, though we are part of the world He came to save, we are not part of the audience to whom His words are addressed. We lack the first condition for understanding what He is talking about. And when men attempt to be Christians without this preliminary consciousness of sin, the result is almost bound to be a certain resentment against God as to one who is always making impossible demands and always inexplicably angry.

                        C. S. LEWIS
                        Mere Christianity

SAFETY IN CHRIST

I give unto them eternal life; and they
shall never perish, neither shall any man
pluck them out of my hand.

                        John 10:28

Unnumber'd years of bliss
I to my sheep will give;
And while my throne unshaken stands
Shall all my chosen live.

> Enough, my gracious Lord,
> Let faith triumphant cry;
> My heart can on this promise live,
> Can with this promise die.
>
> ABRAHAM LINCOLN
> *Devotional*

He lived a perfect life that offered a scant three years of active ministry. He healed the sick, He forgave sins, He taught with shocking authority, He collected a little band of followers, and He offered His life as atonement for sin.

The life of Christ set many patterns for Christians, but it is His death that provides the means by which the example He gave can be followed. Our feet are fallible; only by His help can we walk in His steps.

He said He identified with man as man. He said He identified with God as God. He said He was willing to pay the price for the chasm in between. That's why He died. No one took Christ's life from Him. He gave it away. When Peter urged Him to detour Jerusalem and avoid the threat of death, Christ answered, "It was for this reason I came into the world!" The last words He spoke from the cross were uttered in full control of His senses.

Why was this special One literally born to die? Because God and man had been irrevocably separated by sin. God said He would redeem us from sin, deliver us out from under. That's a phrase from the Bible that eases me everytime I read it:

> . . . I will bring you out from under the
> burdens . . . .
>
> Exodus 6:6

God spelled out the only acceptable sacrifice for sin—that which would deliver us out from under. In the Book of Isaiah, the prophet offers a detailed account of the Messiah's sacrifice.

> . . . and the LORD hath laid on him the
> iniquity of us all.
>
> Isaiah 53:6

The iniquity of us all laid on Him! That's what was so totally finished on the cross. That's why Christ cried out, "It is finished." The full payment for sin rested upon Christ.

And in that moment, Christ, separated from God the Father by our sins, cried out, "My God, My God, why hast Thou forsaken me?" God can have no fellowship with sin, even when it is His only-begotten Son hanging there beneath sin's monstrous burden. That's what Christ did for us. Divine atonement. We accept that when we accept Him as Lord.

JEANNETTE CLIFT

In the Cross of Christ we glory, because we regard it as a matchless exhibition of the attributes of God. We see there the love of God, desiring a way by which He might save mankind, aided by His wisdom, so that a plan is perfected by which the deed can be done without violation of truth and justice. In the Cross we see a strange conjunction of what once appeared to be two opposite qualities—justice and mercy. We see how God is supremely just; as just as if He had no mercy, and yet infinitely merciful in the gift of His Son. Mercy and justice, in fact, become counsel upon the same side, and irresistibly plead for the acquittal of the believing sinner. We can never tell which of the attributes of God shines most glorious in the sacrifice of Christ; they each one find a glorious high throne in the person and work of the Lamb of God, that taketh away the sin of the world. Since it has become, as it were, the disc which reflects the character and perfections of God, it is meet that we should glory in the Cross of Christ, and none shall stay us of our boasting.

CHARLES H. SPURGEON

Forasmuch as ye know that ye were not redeemed with corruptible things, as silver and gold, from your vain conversation received by tradition from your fathers; But with the precious blood of Christ, as of a lamb without blemish and without spot.

1 Peter 1:18, 19

I'm going to heaven and I believe I'm going by the blood of Christ. That's not popular preaching, but I'll tell you it's all the way through the Bible and I may be the last fellow on earth who preaches it, but I'm going to preach it because it's the only way we're going to get there.

BILLY GRAHAM

There is a story about the wife of one of Cyrus's generals who was charged with treachery against the king. She was called before Cyrus and after the trial condemned to die.

Her husband, who did not realize what had taken place, was apprised of it and came hurrying in. When he heard the sentence condemning his wife to death, he threw himself prostrate before the king and said, "O Sire, take my life instead of hers. Let me die in her place!" Cyrus was so touched that he said, "Love like that must not be spoiled by death," and he gave them back to each other and let the wife go free.

As they walked happily away the husband said, "Did you notice how kindly the king looked upon us when he gave you a free pardon?"

"I had no eyes for the king," she said. "I saw only the man who was willing to die for me."

H. A. IRONSIDE

> Jesus now has many lovers of His heavenly Kingdom, but few bearers of His Cross.
>
> THOMAS À KEMPIS

Have you ever watched a fly trying to go straight through a closed window? It flies at the glass again and again, trying to get into the clear air beyond. The fly doesn't know—but you know—that he will never get past that glass unless you take pity on him and open the window.

That must have been how God felt as He watched men flying at the wall they had built between themselves and Him. "They are never going to get past that wall," God must have said, "unless I open a way for them. They are separated from Me, and this separation is death.

"But what if I were to take away this death that follows sin? What if I sent my Son to take this death for men, so that they would not have to die?"

If it seems to be a cruel answer, we must remember that sin is cruel, that what it does to men is cruel, and that to save us from this death, God had to give the very life of His Son. For Jesus is the way that God opened to us, the way back to fellowship with Him.

RUTH BELL GRAHAM
Our Christmas Story

In our scientific age there are thousands
living who owe their lives to blood transfu-
sions. By analogy, it can be reverently said
that, in a mystical sense, the Son of God is
the great universal Donor, giving new life
to the sinner who trusts his shed blood for
cleansing.

L. NELSON BELL

I am crucified with Christ . . . .
Galatians 2:20

The cross of Christ is His greatest glory. Because He humbled Himself
to the death of the cross, therefore God hath highly exalted Him. The
cross was the power that conquered Satan and sin.

The Christian shares with Christ in the cross. The crucified Christ
lives in him through the Holy Spirit, and the spirit of the cross inspires
him. He lives as one who had died with Christ. As he realizes the power
of Christ's crucifixion, he lives as one who has died to the world and to
sin, and the power becomes a reality in his life. It is as the crucified One
that Christ lives in me.

Our Lord said to His disciples: "Take up your cross and follow me."
Did they understand this? They had seen men carrying a cross, and
knew what it meant, a painful death on the cross. And so all His life
Christ bore His cross—the death sentence that He should die for the
world. And each Christian must bear his cross, acknowledging that he is
worthy of death, and believing that he is crucified with Christ, and that
the crucified One lives in him. "Our old man is crucified with Christ."
"He that is Christ's hath crucified the flesh with all the lusts thereof."
When we have accepted this life of the cross, we will be able to say with
Paul: "Far be it from me to glory save in the cross of our Lord Jesus
Christ."

ANDREW MURRAY

I was made to see, again and again, that
God and my soul were friends by His
blood; yea, I saw that the justice of God and
my sinful soul could embrace and kiss each
other, through His blood. This was a good
day to me; I hope I shall never forget it.

JOHN BUNYAN

The people who hanged Christ never accused Him of being a bore—
on the contrary; they thought Him too dynamic to be safe. It has been
left for later generations to muffle up that shattering personality and
surround Him with the atmosphere of tedium. We have very efficiently
pared the claws of the Lion of Judah, certified Him "meek and mild,"
and recommended Him as a fitting household pet for pale curates and
pious old ladies. To those who knew Him, however, He in no way
suggested a milk-and-water person; they objected to Him as a dangerous firebrand. True, He was tender to the unfortunate, patient with
honest inquirers and humble before Heaven; but He insulted respecta-
ble clergymen by calling them hypocrites; He referred to King Herod as
"that fox"; He went to parties in disreputable company and was looked
upon as a "gluttonous man and a winebibber, a friend of publicans and
sinners"; He insulted indignant tradesmen and threw them and their
belongings out of the Temple . . . . He showed no proper deference for
wealth or social position; when confronted with neat dialectical traps,
He displayed a paradoxical humor that affronted serious-minded
people, and He retorted by asking disagreeable questions that could not
be answered by rule of thumb . . . But He had "a daily beauty in His life
that made us ugly," and officialdom felt that the established order of
things would be more secure without Him. So they did away with God
in the name of peace and quietness.

DOROTHY SAYERS

More than nineteen hundred years have passed . . .
The Cross itself has long since crumbled into dust.
Yet, it stands again when we choose our own Calvary and
crucify Him all over again, with every sin of commission
and omission.

>   Every wrong attitude . . .
>   every bad disposition . . .
>   every unkind word . . .
>   every impure imagination . . .
>   every ignoble desire . . .
>   every unworthy ambition . . .

Yes, Calvary still stands, and the crowd at the top
of the hill.

Were you there when they crucified my Lord?
I was . . . Were you?

PETER MARSHALL
"Were You There"

For as the devil through pride led man
from pride to death, so Christ through low-
liness led back man through obedience to
life.

SAINT AUGUSTINE

. . . Since we believe that Christ died for
all of us, we should also believe that we
have died to the old life we used to live. He
died for all so that all who live—having received eternal life from him—might live no
longer for themselves, to please themselves, but to spend their lives pleasing
Christ who died and rose again for them.

2 Corinthians 5:14, 15 LB

LIVINGSTONE'S ANSWER

Christ also hath once suffered for sins,
the just for the unjust, that he might bring
us to God, being put to death in the flesh,
but quickened by the Spirit.

1 Peter 3:18

Ye know that ye were not redeemed with
corruptible things, as silver and gold . . .
But with the precious blood of Christ, as of
a lamb without blemish and without spot.

1 Peter 1:18, 19

When David Livingstone, the great missionary, tried to explain the
philosophy of God's plan of salvation to the Africans, they, hearing the
story for the first time, asked him, "Teacher, how could one man die for
the whole human race?" This is Livingstone's explanation. He dipped
his hand into his pocket and brought out two coins, one a common
British copper penny, the other a little glittering golden sovereign. He
explained that in the country from which he came, the little golden coin,
which was not so large as the penny and did not weigh as much, was
actually worth 240 of the copper pennies. The difference in the value was
a result of the inherent, intrinsic difference in the metal. So he explained
that God's holy, perfect, well-beloved Son was worth a whole world of

guilty, lost, condemned sinners. Our hope for eternity is this—and this alone. My sins deserved eternal death, but Jesus took my place, as He did the places of all others who will receive Him, and "upon Another's life, Another's death, I stake my whole eternity." His precious sacrifice cancels all my debt!

KEITH L. BROOKS

If there be ground for you to trust in your own righteousness, then all that Christ did to purchase salvation, and all that God did to prepare the way for it, is in vain.

JONATHAN EDWARDS

The gift of God is eternal life through Jesus Christ our LORD.

Romans 6:23

A man is saved by trusting in the finished work of Christ on the Cross, and not by bodily sensations and religious ecstasy. But you will say to me, "What about feeling? Is there no place in saving faith for feeling?" Certainly, there is room for feeling in saving faith. But we are not saved by it. Whatever feeling there may be is the result of saving faith, but feeling never saved a single soul. Love is feeling. Joy is feeling. Inward peace is feeling. Love for others is a feeling. Concern for the lost is a feeling. But these feelings are not conversion. The one experience that you can look for and expect is the experience of believing in Christ.

BILLY GRAHAM
Day-by-Day With Billy Graham

If I am not finding Jesus a real Savior, who brings me fully out of darkness and defeat into light and liberty, it is because at one point or another I am not willing to be broken, and see myself as a sinner.

ROY HESSION

Sidney Lanier wrote the following moving poem about Jesus Christ in 1880. It describes the agonizing struggle of our Lord as He prayed in the Garden of Gethsemane, while He awaited His betrayal and arrest. We read of the sacrificial devotion to the will of God as Jesus prayed under the trees, which had often brought Him shade from the searing sun during the day. Then of His ultimate death, which was carried out upon a Cross made from a tree.

Into the woods my Master went,
   Clean forspent, forspent.
Into the woods my Master came,
   Forspent with love and shame.
But the olives they were not blind to Him,
   The little gray leaves were kind to Him,
The thorn-tree had a mind to Him,
   When into the woods He came.

Out of the woods my Master went,
   And He was well content.
Out of the woods my Master came,
   Content with death and shame.
When Death and Shame would woo Him last,
   From under the trees they drew Him last,
'Twas on a tree they slew Him—last
   When out of the woods He came.

SIDNEY LANIER

   We are told that Christ was killed for us,
that his death has washed out our sins, and
that by dying he disabled death itself. Any
theories we build up as to how Christ's
death did all this are, in my view, quite
secondary.

C. S. LEWIS

Jesus and Alexander died at thirty-three.
One died in Babylon, and one on Calvary.
One gained all for himself; and one Himself
   He gave.
One conquered every throne; the other
   every grave.
The one made himself God; the God made
   Himself less.
The one lived but to blast; the other but
   to bless.
When died the Greek, forever fell his
   throne of swords,
But Jesus died to live forever Lord of
   lords.

AUTHOR UNKNOWN

Christ came to reveal what righteousness
really is, for nothing will do except righteousness, and no other conception of righteousness will do except Christ's conception of it—His method and secret.

MATTHEW ARNOLD

One of the Church's most triumphant hymns that describes upon
whom our belief is founded is "The Church's One Foundation." It was
written in 1866 by Samuel J. Stone and is based upon the words of
Jesus—". . . upon this rock I will build my church . . ." (Matthew
16:18). Each time it is sung it reminds us of His love and sacrifice.

The Church's one foundation
  Is Jesus Christ her Lord;
She is His new creation
  By water and the word;
From heaven He came and sought her
  To be His holy Bride;
With His own blood He bought her,
  And for her life He died.

SAMUEL J. STONE

A man may go to heaven without health,
without riches, without honors, without
learning, without friends, but he can never
go there without Christ.

JOHN DYER

INDIFFERENCE

When Jesus came to Golgotha they hanged Him on a tree,
They drave great nails through hands and feet, and made a
      Calvary;
They crowned Him with a crown of thorns, red were His
      wounds and deep,
For those were crude and cruel days, and human flesh was
      cheap.

When Jesus came to our town, they simply passed Him by,
They never hurt a hair of Him, they only let Him die;

For men had grown more tender, and they would not give
    Him pain,
They only just passed down the street, and left Him in
    the rain.

Still Jesus cried, "Forgive them, for they know not what
    they do,"
And still it rained the wintry rain that drenched Him
    through and through;
The crowds went home and left the streets without a soul
    to see,
And Jesus crouched against a wall and cried for Calvary.

                          G. A. STUDDERT-KENNEDY

He taught me all the mercy, for he show'd me all the sin.
Now, tho' my lamp was lighted late, there's One will let
    me in.

                              ALFRED TENNYSON

Jesus Christ never met an unimportant
person. That is why God sent his Son to die
for us. If someone dies for you, you must
be important.

                          M. C. CLEVELAND

A man can accept what Christ has done
without knowing how it works; indeed, he
certainly won't know how it works until
he's accepted it.

                          C. S. LEWIS

Elizabeth C. Clephane knew what it was to suffer intensely, due to ill health. She was only thirty-nine when she died in her native Scotland, but into that short life she brought joy to many of the suffering poor people around her. They called her "Sunbeam."

"Beneath the Cross of Jesus" was written shortly before she died and tells of her confident assurance and trust in Jesus Christ.

Beneath the cross of Jesus
  I fain would take my stand,
The shadow of a mighty Rock
  Within a weary land;
A home within the wilderness,
  A rest upon the way,
From the burning of the noontide heat,
  And the burden of the day.
                    ELIZABETH C. CLEPHANE

Each day I would remember, Lord, the sacrifice that You endured upon the Cross for me. Such love demands my complete devotion. Your wounds remind me of how many times I must still hurt You as often—unthinkingly—I live so selfishly. Thank You, Lord Jesus Christ, for dying for me, even though I do not deserve Your love. Amen.

                                            —J. W. B.

SATURDAY BETWEEN GOOD FRIDAY AND EASTER

That was the Day Between
the Night Before—

The blood
still wet upon the hill;
His body
wrapped,
entombed,
and still;
the great stone sealed
with Roman seal
and guarded well.

Many a Judean home
had now become
a lesser tomb
within whose walls
men lay,
whose Life had died
That Day.

Looking back
we cannot share
their black
despair.

For us
He is the Risen Christ,
as He had said:
for them, that Shabbat,
all life died—
for He was dead.
       *   *   *
That was the Day Between
the Night Before.
       *   *   *
This is my Day Between,
my Night Before . . .

Suspended
in this interim—
let me be still,
let me adore,
let me remember
Him.

RUTH BELL GRAHAM
*Sitting by My
Laughing Fire*

Jesus—His Resurrection

Our Shared Triumph

The Resurrection never becomes a fact of experience until the risen Christ lives in the heart of the believer.

PETER MARSHALL

Imagine the despair of Jesus' disciples! They had seen their beloved Lord die the most cruel and ignominious death. In almost uncontrollable grief they had gently taken Him down from the Cross and placed Him in a tomb carved out of rock. They had watched while a great boulder was rolled across the opening, with unrelenting finality. A finality that so many experience when they attend a loved one's funeral.

Fear and despair were their companions. All their hope was shattered—there was nothing for them to live for. The cause of Christianity was dead.

In the Apostles' Creed it says that He "was crucified, dead and buried." Could anything sound more final, more hopeless?

How beautiful are the following words, from the same Creed. "The third day He rose again from the dead; He ascended into heaven, and sitteth on the right hand of God the Father Almighty."

The knocking on the door and Mary Magdalene's urgent voice awakened the disciples out of their despair, as she told them that she had seen the Lord—that He had risen as He said He would! What joy, doubt, excitement must have crowded into their minds as they ran back to the garden, where the tomb was, and saw with their own eyes that the stone had been rolled away and that the tomb was empty! No gravestone would ever be inscribed HERE LIES JESUS CHRIST for He was *alive!*

What a difference this makes for you and me, for it means we never have to fear death—our Saviour has conquered it. ". . . because I live, ye shall live also'' (John 14:19). It means that through Him we shall know immortality and that when we stand at the graveside of a loved one it is *not* the end, for those who love Him. He has promised that He has gone on to prepare a place for us.

Christians all over the world will testify to the truth of Christ's Resurrection, for they sense His presence with them—the Living Risen Lord. It is the same Lord that walked in the cool of the garden that first Easter morning and spoke Mary's name. He speaks our names today, for He loves us and longs for our companionship too.

Each time we see the empty Cross let it remind us of the suffering of Jesus, but also the *victory*. In the words of Peter Marshall, "Let us never live another day as if *He* were dead!"

—*J. W. B.*

> The rock . . .
> The Roman lock . . .
> What is there to it?
> How did he do it?
>
> They tell me he is risen
> Out of death's prison
> But how can that be?
> What did they see?
>
> O terror of that daybreak hour
> O rapture of the Savior's power,
> O Life that broke but did not bend,
> O grave that burst from end to end!

You are a temple guard in Jerusalem. You have been losing sleep for some days. There was the affair Thursday night—the arrest, the questioning, and general disorder. Friday night you were assigned to guard a tomb in the garden of Joseph of Arimathaea, and you are still there. It is now early Sunday morning, and you have settled back against a nearby rock to steal forty winks. You have a dream: a mighty angel appears before you with feet widespread. He raises his arm and places a golden trumpet to his lips, and there issues forth a blast that shatters the air and causes the earth beneath you to tremble. You waken in a sweat, fearing the end of everything. All is quiet; your comrades are drowsing. Then you peer through the gray murk at the tomb that is your responsibility. Something about it seems to be different. You rub your eyes, get up, and walk toward it, only to stop amazed at the sight of the broken seal. The stone has been rolled aside. For a moment you are shocked into rigidity. Then you shout, you summon the guard, and there ensues—pandemonium!

You have been the first to witness the power of the Resurrection.

SHERWOOD ELIOT WIRT
The Cross on the Mountain

In the end of the sabbath, as it began to dawn toward the first day of the week, came Mary Magdalene and the other Mary to see the sepulchre.

And, behold . . . the angel of the LORD descended from heaven, and came and rolled back the stone from the door . . . .

And the angel . . . said unto the women, Fear not ye: for I know that ye seek Jesus, which was crucified.

He is not here: for he is risen, as he said. Come, see the place where the LORD lay.

And go quickly, and tell his disciples that he is risen from the dead; and, behold, he goeth before you into Galilee; there shall ye see him . . . .

Matthew 28:1, 2; 5–7

The stone was rolled away from the door,
not to permit Christ to come out, but to
enable the disciples to go in.

PETER MARSHALL

"I KNOW THAT MY REDEEMER LIVETH"

They asked me how I know it's true
That the Saviour lived and died . . .
And if I believe the story
That the Lord was crucified?
And I have so many answers
To prove His Holy Being.
Answers that are everywhere
Within the realm of seeing . . .
The leaves that fell at Autumn
And were buried in the sod
Now budding on the tree boughs
To lift their arms to God . . .

The flowers that were covered
And entombed beneath the snow
Pushing through the "darkness"
To bid the Spring "hello" . . .
On every side Great Nature
Retells the Easter Story—
So who am I to question
"The Resurrection Glory."

HELEN STEINER RICE

The first to see Jesus after His death was Mary Magdalene. The greatest news that ever broke upon the world, the news which was to change the whole life of humanity and shake down thrones and revolutionise kingdoms, the news which still to-day girdles the earth with everlasting hope and sends a new thrill through every Christian soul on Easter morning, was given first to one humble, obscure woman out of whom seven devils had gone, who had nothing to distinguish her but her forgiven heart, and no claim at all but her love. Mary had come out, before dawn was in the sky, to sit beside a dead body. She was telling herself that everything else but that was gone—the voice of Jesus that would never speak again, the light in those eyes that would shine no more, the living soul that was fled for ever—all gone, and only the dead body left for love and gratitude to cling to and try to serve. She came, and even that was gone. This was her moment of final desolation. "They have taken away my Lord, and I know not where they have laid Him." Blinded with tears, her eyes could not recognize Someone standing near, but He called her by her name, and then she knew. "Jesus saith unto her, Mary. She turned herself, and saith unto Him, Rabboni; which is to say, Master." What she had once been saved from and forgiven was the measure of her devotion; and always it is those who love Jesus best, who see Him first.

JAMES S. STEWART

HE IS RISEN!

Why do you look
for the living
among
the
dead?
He is not here:
he has been raised!

Remember what he said to you,
 while he was still in Galilee—
  that the Son of Man must be betrayed into the hands
  of sinful men,
   and must be crucified,
   and must rise again on the third day.
                                    Luke 24:5–7 PHILLIPS

For each of us there is a very short time during which we can use our words, our influence, or our prayer times to help others to be in the right place or to have the true motive for their search. It was not long after the soldiers in the Garden had found Jesus, only a long weekend later, that Mary weepingly sought Him. He had been hung on the cross. He had died. Her weeping was with desolate loneliness and disappointment and fear. She was seeking her Lord's dead body with sorrow, love, honesty, but also with depression. No thought of life in her words to the gardener. "[Then] Jesus said unto her, Woman, why weepest thou? whom *seekest* thou? . . ." (John 20:15). She supposed He was a gardener and wanted to know where her Lord's body was, and then the living, resurrected Jesus spoke in accent and tone that she recognized with a sharp remembrance. "Mary . . ." and her reply was "Master." She had found Him. She had found her risen Lord in a body which she would be able to touch after He ascended to His Father, and her Father, His God and her God. And she believed. She went to the others to tell them that she had seen the Lord. He was alive. One day—if we have found Him as our Saviour and Lord, our Atonement and our God—we will talk to Mary—alive forevermore in her resurrected body, as we are in ours.

                                    EDITH SCHAEFFER

The glorious fact that the empty tomb pro-
claims to us is that life for us does not stop
when death comes.

Death is not a wall, but a door.

And eternal life which may be ours now,
by faith in Christ, is not interrupted when
the soul leaves the body,
 for we live on . . . and on.

There is no death to those who have entered
into fellowship with Him who emerged from
the tomb.

Because the Resurrection is true, it is the
most significant thing in our world today.
Bringing the Resurrected Christ into our
lives, individual and national, is the only
hope we have for making a better world.

"Because I live, ye shall live also."

That is the message of Easter.
                    PETER MARSHALL
                    "The Verdict of the Empty Tomb"

There are many historical facts in the world that were not attended by
one-tenth as many witnesses as was the Resurrection of Jesus Christ. As
examples, I might speak of the birth of princes, the signing of treaties,
the remarks of cabinet officers, and the deeds of assassins. I say these
great events that men receive upon testimony and accept as facts, these
have not had one-tenth the number of witnesses as had the Resurrection
of Jesus Christ. Therefore I need not beg anybody's pardon for what I
believe. I believe with all my heart that Jesus, the Christ, is risen indeed.
I believe that He was seen after His Resurrection, by 641 eye witnesses.
During those forty days, Jesus appeared to different men under different
circumstances at various places. He ate with them, walked with them,
and talked with them. They positively could not have been deceived.
Such deception would be without parallel in history and without an
analogy in the annals of men. Christ's enemies became the charter
members of His church, in Jerusalem on the day of Pentecost. Account
for that fact if you deny the Resurrection.
                                        CHARLES R. SCOVILLE

HOPE

He died!
And with Him perished all that men hold dear;
Hope lay beside Him in the sepulcher,
Love grew corpse cold, and all things beautiful beside
        Died when He did.
                He rose!

And with Him hope arose, and life and light.
Men said, "Not Christ but Death died yesternight."
And joy and truth and all things virtuous
    Rose when He rose.

AUTHOR UNKNOWN

    The most important events in human history are the death and resurrection of Jesus Christ.

BILLY GRAHAM

Easter day breaks!
Christ rises! Mercy every way is infinite—
Earth breaks up; time drops away;
In flows heaven with its new day
Of endless life—
What is left for us save in growth
Of soul to rise up . . .
From the gift looking to the giver,
And from the cistern to the river,
And from the finite to infinity,
And from man's dust to God's divinity.

ROBERT BROWNING

AN EASTER WISH

May the glad dawn
    Of Easter morn
    Bring joy to thee.

May the calm eve
    Of Easter leave
    A peace divine with thee.

May Easter night
    On thine heart write,
    O Christ, I live for Thee!

AUTHOR UNKNOWN

It is on the unshakable fact of the resurrection of Christ from the dead that I base
my faith in God's utter integrity and faith-
fulness. He let Jesus die—but only because
he would raise him again. You can count
on him! You can stake your faith on God—
the God of Jesus Christ. He will keep his
word.

LEIGHTON FORD

Our Lord has written the promise of the
Resurrection, not in books alone, but in
every leaf in springtime.

MARTIN LUTHER

The miracle of Christ's resurrection: out
of the grave into my heart.

DAVID J. NETZ

THE EMPTY TOMB

It was the third day, the day Jesus said He would arise. Around the
tomb the earth began to shake, and along with it the armor of the Roman
soldiers must have clattered wildly. And then an angel of the Lord came
from heaven and easily rolled away the stone and sat on it . . . The
guards just looked at him and became like dead men. The angel spoke to
Mary Magdalene and Mary, too, but the Bible says that they took action
and ran to tell the disciples that He had risen.

When Peter and John came running to the tomb, John peeped in and
saw the linen clothes Christ had been wrapped in lying there empty.
Peter, who, true to his character, blundered right in, saw that Jesus'
body was missing. He was gone.

The bodily resurrection was a fact attested to by hundreds of eyewit-
nesses. We have records of thirteen different appearances of Jesus under
widely different circumstances. His body was both similar and dissimi-
lar to the one nailed to the cross. It was so similar to an ordinary human
body that Mary mistook Him for the caretaker of the garden by the tomb
when He appeared to her. He could eat, speak to people, and occupy
space.

However, His body was not like a normal body. He could pass

through closed doors or vanish in a moment. Christ's body was physical, and also spiritual. Why should this be surprising? Paul said to King Agrippa, "Why should it be thought a thing incredible with you, that God should raise the dead?" (Acts 26:8).

Over and over again the Bible affirms the fact of the bodily resurrection of Christ. Luke says it very directly in the Book of Acts. He reports that Jesus "presented Himself alive, after His suffering, by many convincing proofs, appearing to them over a period of forty days" (Acts 1:3).

In speaking about those "convincing proofs," C. S. Lewis says, "The first fact in the history of Christendom is a number of people who say they have seen the Resurrection. If they had died without making anyone else believe this 'gospel' no gospels would ever have been written."

BILLY GRAHAM
How to Be Born Again

. . . By [God's] great mercy we have been born anew to a living hope through the resurrection of Jesus Christ from the dead, and to an inheritance which is imperishable, undefiled, and unfading, kept in heaven for you.

1 Peter 1:3, 4 RSV

The records represent Christ as passing after death (as no man had passed before) neither into a purely, that is, negatively, "spiritual" mode of existence nor into a "natural" life such as we know, but into a life which has its own, new Nature. It represents Him as withdrawing six weeks later, into some different mode of existence. It says—He says—that He goes "to prepare a place for us." This presumably means that He is about to create that whole new Nature which will provide the environment or conditions for His glorified humanity and, in Him, for ours. The picture is not what we expected—though whether it is less or more probable and philosophical on that account is another question. It is not the picture of an escape from any and every kind of Nature into some unconditioned and utterly transcendent life. It is the picture of a new human nature, and a new Nature in general, being brought into existence. We must, indeed, believe the risen body to be extremely different from the mortal body: but the existence, in that new state, of anything that could in any sense be described as "body" at all, involves some sort of spatial relations and in the long run a whole new universe. That is the picture—not of unmaking but of remaking. The old field of space, time, matter, and the senses is to be weeded, dug, and sown for a new crop. We may be tired of that old field: God is not.

C. S. LEWIS
Miracles

MY RISEN LORD

My risen Lord, I feel Thy strong protection;
I see Thee stand among the graves today;
"I am the Way, the Life, the Resurrection,"
    I hear Thee say,
And all the burdens I have carried sadly
Grow light as blossoms on an April day;
My cross becomes a staff; I journey gladly
    This Easter Day.

AUTHOR UNKNOWN

On which side of Easter are you living? Are you on the dark, dreary, defeated side, where the powers of evil still reign and death still has the final word? Or are you living on the blessed, beautiful side of the resurrection, with an assurance that Christ has won, death has been defeated, and eternal life has begun in a way that no mere cessation of physical life can hinder?

Jesus Christ said, "I am the resurrection and the life; he who lives and believes in me shall never die." But he followed this profound statement with a penetrating question: "Do you believe this?" (John 11:25.)

LLOYD JOHN OGILVIE
The Cup of Wonder

Then he [Jesus] said to Thomas, "Put your finger into my hands. Put your hand into my side. Don't be faithless any longer. Believe!"
"My Lord and my God!" Thomas said.

John 20:27, 28 LB

That the Resurrection happened, and that in consequence of it Jesus' followers who had scattered drew together again, resolved to go about their Master's business, seems to me indubitably true. Likewise, Jesus' claim to be the Light of the World, and his related promise that through him we may be reborn into new men, liberated from servitude to the ego and our appetites into the glorious liberty of the children of God. Compared with these tremendous certainties, dubieties about the precise circumstances of Jesus' birth, ministry, death on the Cross and continuing presence in the world, seem sterile and unprofitable. Either Jesus never was or he still is. As a typical product of these confused times, with a sceptical mind and a sensual disposition, diffidently and unworthily, but with the utmost certainty, I assert that he still is. If the story of Jesus had ended on Golgotha, it would indeed be of a Man Who Died, but as two thousand years later the Man's promise that *where two or three are gathered together in my name, there am I in the midst of them*, manifestly still holds, it is actually the story of a Man Who Lives.

MALCOLM MUGGERIDGE

If you confess with your lips that Jesus is LORD and believe in your heart that God raised him from the dead, you will be saved. For man believes with his heart and so is justified, and he confesses with his lips and so is saved.

Romans 10:9, 10 RSV

Blessed be the God and Father of our Lord Jesus Christ, which according to his abundant mercy hath begotten us again unto a lively hope by the resurrection of Jesus Christ from the dead, To an inheritance incorruptible, and undefiled, and that fadeth not away, reserved in heaven for you.

1 Peter 1:3, 4

There *is* evidence for the deity of Jesus—good, strong, historical, cumulative evidence; evidence to which an honest person can subscribe without committing intellectual suicide. There are the extravagant claims which Jesus made for himself, so bold and yet so unassuming. Then there is his incomparable character. His strength and gentleness, his uncompromising righteousness and tender compassion, his care for children and his love for outcasts, his self-mastery and self-sacrifice have won the admiration of the world. What is more, his cruel death was not the end of him. It is claimed that he rose again from death, and the circumstantial evidence for his resurrection is most compelling.

Supposing Jesus was the Son of God, is basic Christianity merely an acceptance of this fact? No. Once persuaded of the deity of his person, we must examine the nature of his work. What did he come to do? The biblical answer is, he "came into the world to save sinners." Jesus of Nazareth is the heaven-sent Saviour we sinners need. We need to be forgiven and restored to fellowship with the all-holy God, from whom our sins have separated us. We need to be set free from our selfishness and given strength to live up to our ideals. We need to learn to love one another, friend and foe alike. This is the meaning of "salvation." This is what Christ came to win for us by his death and resurrection.

JOHN R. W. STOTT

From this moment, O living Christ, we ask Thee to go with us wherever we go; be our Companion in all that we do. And for this greatest of all gifts, we offer Thee our sacrifices of thanksgiving. *Amen.*

PETER MARSHALL
The Prayers of Peter Marshall

The resurrection of Jesus stands fast as a fact, unaffected by the waves of skepticism that ceaselessly through the ages beat themselves against it. It holds within it the vastest hope for time and eternity that humanity can ever know.

JAMES ORR

OUR CHRIST

I know not how that Bethlehem's Babe
   Could in the God-head be;
I only know the Manger Child
   Has brought God's life to me.

I know not how that Calvary's cross
   A world from sin could free:
I only know its matchless love
   Has brought God's love to me.

I know not how that Joseph's tomb
   Could solve death's mystery:
I only know a living Christ,
   Our immortality.

HARRY WEBB FARRINGTON

They had heard the reports of the appearance of Jesus to His disciples by the Sea of Tiberius; and of how He had appeared to others on a mountain in Galilee. More, they had heard over and over again the story, incredible to them both, of how Jesus had gathered all His loved ones around Him on the top of Mount Olivet, had promised them—"Lo, I am with you always, even until the consummation of the world"—and then had visibly departed heavenward until He was hidden and lost in clouds.

Now, in the moist warmth of the torrid night, Annas and Caiphas sat together in the dark, remembering so much of this man whom they had ordered killed yet who still could plague their peace of mind.

"The reason I came here tonight," explained Caiphas, "is that we shall have to agree on a strong policy."

"You still want action? More action?"

"Yes."

Annas clucked his tongue and lips together.

"But I thought you had already started on this sort of thing without bothering to consult me. Haven't I heard that you had a young man named Stephen brought up on charges? Wasn't he a follower of Jesus? Did you have a lot of trouble with him?"

"We condemned him, too."

"Yes, and you stoned him to death, and the followers of Jesus now declare that he is a martyr—the first from among themselves."

"Perhaps he will not be the last."

"But has it occurred to you, Caiphas, that this brave death contradicts all that you had to say earlier this evening? Would any man be willing to die—in a heroic, glorious martyrdom like this—for some conjurer's trick involving the stealing of a corpse in a hoax, a sham? No! He was one of the men present when they say Jesus showed them hands, feet, and the wound in His side."

"I still don't see—"

"Probably you never will. But I shall try to give you a gleam of light. On the night we killed Him, you remember that two of His disciples followed Him into Jerusalem but one of them denied Him three times and both kept themselves hidden. What happened to the other nine? They couldn't get away fast enough. They went back to Galilee where they came from, and glad enough to get there. Why? Because they were afraid. They had pretended all along to themselves that they believed He was the Messiah—and maybe they did—but when they came to face danger they lost faith and ran."

"Cowards as well as fools!" fleered Caiphas.

"But what makes them brave now?" asked Annas sternly. "How is it a man can die so willingly? All the others, preaching today on the streets of Jerusalem, know that their ultimate fate is violent death. They know what they stand for and what you stand for, Caiphas, and they know this world will always be a place of fear, of want, of war, of all kinds of suffering, as long as those two conflicting points of view exist. The world will be a better place, Caiphas, only when their side wins. And they *will* win. We can only kill them; but they can conquer us.

"Why do they no longer care whether they live or die? Because they have seen their leader rise from the dead; they expect to do the same; to them, now, life and death are mere words for temporary things and do not really matter. Since the resurrection, that is what is means to be a Christian."

FULTON OURSLER

> Christ is alive. To thousands upon thousands at the present hour this is no mere theory or vague, uncertain rumour, but proved, inviolable experience; and if they

are facing life victoriously now where once
they were defeated, it is because they have
found the same Risen Lord who walked
among the flowers of the garden on the
morning of the first Easter day.

JAMES S. STEWART

Were you there when they crucified my Lord?
Were you there when they crucified my Lord?
Oh! sometimes it causes me to tremble, tremble, tremble.
Were you there when they crucified my Lord?

Were you there when they pierced Him in the side?
Were you there when they pierced Him in the side?
Oh! sometimes it causes me to tremble, tremble, tremble.
Were you there when they pierced Him in the side?

Were you there when they laid Him in the tomb?
Were you there when they laid Him in the tomb?
Oh! sometimes it causes me to tremble, tremble, tremble.
Were you there when they laid Him in the tomb?

Were you there when He rose from the dead?
Were you there when He rose from the dead?
Oh! sometimes it causes me to tremble, tremble, tremble.
Were you there when He rose from the dead?

Were you there when He ascended on high?
Were you there when He ascended on high?
Oh! sometimes it causes me to tremble, tremble, tremble.
Were you there when He ascended on high?

A spiritual

And he led them out as far as to Bethany, and he lifted
        up his hands, and blessed them.
And it came to pass, while he blessed them, he was parted
        from them, and carried up into heaven.
And they worshipped him, and returned to Jerusalem with
        great joy.

Luke 24:50–52

And He departed from our sight that we might return to our heart, and there find Him. For He departed, and behold, He is here.

SAINT AUGUSTINE

. . . and, lo, I am with you alway, even unto the end of the world.

Matthew 28:20

Oh, Risen Lord, You have brought hope and broken the shadows of the bleakness of death! As You appeared in the garden to Mary to tell of Your triumph over our last enemy, You speak to us now— consoling—helping us to realize that death is the beginning of a glorious eternity with You! Amen.

—J. W. B.

Jesus—His Return

Our Daily Hope

There is coming a day that will be called the Day of the Lord.
In the midst of hopelessness there is hope! And that hope is
centered in the God-man, the Lord Jesus Christ.

BILLY GRAHAM

How often we long for a world without war, hatred, or greed. Each day as we read the newspapers or watch television, it appears that everything is escalating so fast, and there is no answer to the manifold problems that surround us. But beyond all this heartache there is an expectation—a promise that is going to be fulfilled—Jesus' return!

If our hope is based on earthly things, then we are bound to be disappointed and fearful. But to those of us who have experienced Jesus Christ's presence, we can live each day with hope in our hearts; knowing that whatever happens, when the time is perfect, as God has planned, His Son will return to rule this world.

> And the stars of heaven shall fall, and the pow-
> ers that are in heaven shall be shaken. And then
> shall they see the Son of man coming in the
> clouds with great power and glory.
>
> Mark 13:25, 26

When we anticipate seeing someone we love, who has been separated from us, how wonderful it is to know that we are going to be with that person again. We have so much to look forward to—there is something in the future that is going to bring us happiness. The *great* promise is that each day we can expect Jesus to return—we should always have that expectancy, that hope of seeing Him.

I often meet people who say, "Life is meaningless and empty. I have nothing to look forward to." I can empathize with these people, for once I felt like they do. Then the Living Christ came into my life and brought His joy. Now, no matter what problems there are to face, no matter how desperate the situation, there is the underlying knowledge that He is with me and one day I shall see Him face-to-face!

Life is no longer meaningless with Jesus Christ! His anticipated return is *fact*. Because of this, there are questions that none of us can avoid, if we want to be ready for His arrival:

Is He Master and Lord of my life?

Will we be ready for that day when "every knee shall bow"?

—*J. W. B.*

When the Son of man comes in his glory, and all the angels with him, then he will sit on his glorious throne. Before him will be gathered all the nations, and he will separate them one from another as a shepherd separates the sheep from the goats, and he will place the sheep at his right hand, but the goats at the left.

Then the King will say to those at his right hand, "Come, O blessed of my Father, inherit the kingdom prepared for you from the foundation of the world; for I was hungry and you gave me food, I was thirsty and you gave me drink, I was a stranger and you welcomed me, I was naked and you clothed me, I was sick and you visited me. I was in prison and you came to me." Then the righteous will answer him, "LORD, when did we see thee hungry and feed thee, or thirsty and give thee drink? And when did we see thee a stranger and welcome thee, or naked and clothe thee? And when did we see thee sick or in prison and visit thee?" And the King will answer them, "Truly, I say to you, as you did it to one of the least of these my brethren, you did it to me."

Matthew 25:31–40 RSV

One of the best ways to get rid of discouragement is to remember that Christ is coming again. The most thrilling, glorious truth in all the world is the second coming of Jesus Christ. When we look about today and see pessimism on every side, we should remember the Bible is the only book in the world that predicts the future. The Bible is more modern than tomorrow morning's newspaper. The Bible accurately foretells the future, and it says that the consummation of all things shall be the coming again of Jesus Christ to this earth. If your life is dismal, depressed, and gloomy today, Christ can turn those dark clouds inside out. The sunlight of His love can still shine into the darkest part of your life.

BILLY GRAHAM
Day-by-Day With Billy Graham

Face-to-face with Christ my Savior,
Face-to-face—what will it be—
When with rapture I behold Him,
Jesus Christ who died for me?

Face-to-face I shall behold Him,
Far beyond the starry sky;
Face-to-face in all His glory,
I shall see Him by and by!

CARRIE E. BECK

The Second Advent is possible any day,
impossible no day.

RICHARD TRENCH

There is peace in heaven, peace purchased by the blood of his cross. There is peace in the hearts of his people who have come to that cross and experienced his salvation. But there will be no peace on earth until he returns and establishes his kingdom. "Of the increase of his government and peace there shall be no end, upon the throne of David, and upon his kingdom, to order it, and to establish it with judgment and with justice from henceforth even for ever. The zeal of the Lord of hosts will perform this" (Isaiah 9:7).

It is then that the great promises of peace found in the prophets will all be fulfilled. The lion will lie down with the lamb. The nations will beat their swords into plowshares. Men will study war no more.

Meanwhile, we wait for his coming. And as we wait, we enjoy his peace and we share his peace with a troubled world around us. We love him; we labor for him; we look for him. We long for that day when he shall reign, and when the breathtaking promises of Psalm 72 will be fulfilled: "The mountains shall bring peace to the people, and the little hills, by righteousness . . . He shall come down like rain upon the mown grass: as showers that water the earth. In his days shall the righteous flourish; and abundance of peace so long as the moon endureth" (verses 3, 6, 7).

Even so, come quickly, Lord Jesus!

WARREN W. WIERSBE

We are not a postwar generation, but a
pre-peace generation. Jesus is coming.

CORRIE TEN BOOM

Christ designed that the day of His coming should be hid from us, that being in suspense, we might be as it were upon the watch.

MARTIN LUTHER

What did He say?

First He says it one way, and then He says it the other. "A little while, and you will not see me, and again a little while, and you will see me" (*see* John 16:19).

Well, which is it going to be? Will I see Him or won't I see Him? Doesn't Jesus know?

Or is He too clear? I mean, so clear that at first I miss the meaning of what He says?

He was talking to His followers, those who knew Him best—the disciples. And He told them: I'm going to the Father. In a little while I'm leaving. I'll be gone from this earth.

But I'm not going to be away forever. It won't be too long. In fact, just a little while, and I'll be back. You'll see Me again.

The disciples were there with Him when He said it; He hadn't left them yet. They couldn't possibly have understood what that second part meant—"again a little while, and you will see me"—because He hadn't gone yet.

But I know what He meant, being here during the in-between times, walking with Him by faith, and longing to know Him by sight.

Those words probably didn't hit the disciples like they hit me: "You will see me."

Jesus must have been looking down the line a little at us, the waiting ones, because after He said that, He added those five additional words: "And your hearts will rejoice" (*see* John 16:22).

He's right; they will.

ROGER C. PALMS

I know that my redeemer lives, and at last he will stand upon the earth.

Job 19:25 RSV

Have we not seen Thy shining garment's hem
Floating at dawn across the golden skies,
Through thin blue veils at noon, bright majesties,
Seen starry hosts delight to gem
The splendour that shall be Thy diadem?

O Immanence, that knows nor far nor near,
But as the air we breathe is with us here,
Our Breath of Life, O Lord, we worship Thee.

Worship and laud and praise Thee evermore,
Look up in wonder, and behold a door
Opened in heaven, and One set on a throne;
Stretch out a hand, and touch Thine own,
O Christ, our King, our Lord whom we adore.

AMY CARMICHAEL

What is our hope, or joy, or crown of
rejoicing? Are not even ye in the presence
of our Lord Jesus Christ at his coming?
1 Thessalonians 2:19

All hail the power of Jesus' name!
    Let angels prostrate fall;
Bring forth the royal diadem
    And crown Him Lord of all!
Bring forth the royal diadem
    And crown Him Lord of all!

Let every kindred, every tribe
    On this terrestrial ball
To Him all majesty ascribe
    And crown Him Lord of all!
To Him all majesty ascribe
    And crown Him Lord of all!

Oh, that with yonder sacred throng
    We at His feet may fall,
Join in the everlasting song
    And crown Him Lord of all!
Join in the everlasting song
    And crown Him Lord of all!

EDWARD PERRONET

LIVES A LIFE OF HOPE

Looking for the mercy of our Lord Jesus
Christ unto eternal life.

Jude 21.

Rejoice in glorious hope;
    Jesus, the Judge, shall come,
And take his servants up
    To their eternal home:
Lift up your heart, lift up your voice;
Rejoice, he bids his saints rejoice.

ABRAHAM LINCOLN
Devotional

He was God in the person of His Son, come to take away the sins of the world, to bear our griefs and carry our sorrows, to be wounded for our transgressions and bruised for our iniquities; for the sins of men He was to be stricken, and God in infinite love and compassion was to lay on His sinless body the iniquity of us all.

There is a new note of gladness to "Joy to the World" when we look beyond the Bethlehem fields to Calvary, and then on to the mount across the Kidron in the east—when, knowing that He has saved us from our sins, we hear the words of angels again: "This same Jesus . . . shall so come in like manner," and know that at that time we will meet Him in the glorious company of the redeemed.

L. NELSON BELL

Of one thing I am certain: the One who
started the good work in you will bring it to
completion by the Day of Christ Jesus.

Philippians 1:6 NEW ENGLISH BIBLE

There's a light upon the mountains,
    And the day is at the spring,
When our eyes shall see the beauty
    And the glory of the King:
Weary was our heart with waiting,
    And the night-watch seemed so long,
But His triumph-day is breaking,
    And we hail it with a song . . . .

He is breaking down the barriers,
  He is casting up the way;
He is calling for His angels
  To build up the gates of day:
But His angels here are human,
  Not the shining hosts above;
For the drum-beats of His army
  Are the heart-beats of our love.

Hark! we hear a distant music,
  And it comes with fuller swell;
'Tis the triumph-song of Jesus,
  Of our King, Immanuel!

HENRY BURTON

So often we talk about the second coming of Christ as if He is helpless until then. My dear friends, Christ is here now. That is what makes the Christian faith so different from every other religion. Our Lord is not One who merely once lived and told us how to live. He lives now. The Christian shrine is not at a grave in some garden. That grave is empty—deserted.

When He ascended into heaven, the disciples did not feel left alone. As Dr. Malty said, "It was expedient that He go out of some men's sight in order to be near to all men's hearts." Whatever your need, He can meet it. His power is sufficient.

CHARLES L. ALLEN

Synchronize your watch with heaven's clock. You can do that by reading the Bible together with the newspaper. Then you will know that we live in the time when we can expect Jesus' coming again to earth very soon. Listen closely to what the Lord is willing to tell you. The Holy Spirit can make your prayer and conversation with Himself a joyful speaking and listening.

CORRIE TEN BOOM
Each New Day

THE MORNING BREAKS

Beyond the war-clouds and the reddened ways,
I see the Promise of the Coming Days!
I see His Sun arise, new charged with grace
Earth's tears to dry and all her woes efface!
Christ lives! Christ loves! Christ rules!
No more shall Might,
Though leagued with all the Forces of the Night,
Ride over Right. No more shall Wrong
The world's gross agonies prolong.
Who waits His Time shall surely see
The triumph of His Constancy;—
When without let, or bar, or stay,
The coming of His Perfect Day
Shall sweep the Powers of Night away;—
And Faith, replumed for nobler flight,
And Hope, aglow with radiance bright,
And Love, in loveliness bedight,
Shall greet the morning light!

JOHN OXENHAM

The fact of Jesus' coming is the final and
unanswerable proof that God cares.

WILLIAM BARCLAY

Since Jesus came the first time, the world has been "changing administrations." Jesus has won "all authority" by his death and resurrection, but he is not yet exercising that authority completely. Sin, death, evil, and the devil still have a little breathing space, a little time left. But though all do not realize it, Jesus is Lord, and when someday he comes back, every knee shall bow and every tongue confess that Jesus Christ is Lord, to the glory of God the Father!

LEIGHTON FORD

For God so loved the world
  He gave His only Son,
To die on Calvary's tree,
  From sin to set me free;
Some day He's coming back,
  What glory that will be!
Wonderful His love to me.

FRANCES TOWNSEND

Beloved, now are we the sons of God,
and it doth not yet appear what we shall be:
but we know that, when he shall appear,
we shall be like him; for we shall see him as
he is.

1 John 3:2

THE ETERNAL WORD

In the beginning was the Word;
  Athwart the Chaos, night;
It gleamed with quick creative power
  And there was life and light.

Thy Word, O God, is living yet
  Amid earth's restless strife,
New harmony creating still
  And ever higher life.

O Word that broke the stillness first,
  Sound on, and never cease
Till all earth's darkness be made light,
  And all her discord peace.

Till selfish passion, strife and wrong,
  Thy summons shall have heard,
And Thy creation be complete,
  O Thou Eternal Word.

HENRY WADSWORTH LONGFELLOW

Whatever resistance we see today offered
by almost all the world to the progress of
the truth, we must not doubt that our Lord
will come at last to break through all the
undertakings of men and make a passage
for His Word.

JOHN CALVIN

Make a joyful noise unto the Lord, all the earth;
Break forth and sing for joy, yea, sing praises.
Let the sea roar, and the fullness thereof:
The world, and they that dwell therein:
Let the floods clap their hands;
Let the hills sing for joy together
Before the Lord; for He cometh to judge the earth:
He will judge the world with righteousness,
And the people with equity.

ISAAC WATTS

KING OF KINGS

I beheld, and I heard the voice of many
angels round about the throne and the
[creatures] and the elders: and the number
of them was ten thousand times ten thousand, and thousands of thousands; Saying
with a loud voice, Worthy is the Lamb that
was slain to receive power, and riches, and
wisdom, and strength, and honour, and
glory, and blessing.

Revelation 5:11, 12

It is recorded of Queen Victoria, that in the year of her coronation she
attended a public performance of Handel's oratorio *The Messiah*. She had
been instructed by her court advisers that whereas the audience would
rise and remain standing when the "Hallelujah Chorus" was sung, it
was the royal prerogative to remain seated. So when the chorus began,
those in the vast audience rose to their feet. At first there was a struggle
in the Queen's mind between the wish to observe court etiquette and
the instincts of her heart, which moved her to honor the Lord she loved.
When the choir sang the inspiring passage King of kings, and Lord of

lords, the Queen rose to her feet and stood in the royal box, thus bearing witness to Christ her Lord. It was only what might have been expected from devout Queen Victoria. There are times when the pent-up flood of emotion of every spiritual nature must burst open the sluice gates or overflow the barriers of social customs and human restraints. Let us on every possible occasion give honor to Him who has redeemed us by His precious blood, not fearing to confess His Name.

KEITH L. BROOKS

"Oh, I wish He would come today, so that I could lay my crowns at His feet!"

QUEEN VICTORIA

A five-year-old recently was in the bedroom with her little brother when he died at three and a half, choking with croup. "Mother, Mother. He has gone. I'm alone. Philippe has gone." Although she had never seen death before, this little girl recognized that Philippe had left—had gone away, was no longer there in that location anymore. Gone where? What destination is ahead when people go in this way? Is there a specific destination? Is there a place? Can one be absolutely sure of arriving when the time comes to go out of the body, to somewhere else?

The Lord Jesus was speaking directly to that haunting fear when He said so clearly, "Let not your heart be troubled: ye believe in God, believe also in me. In my Father's house are many mansions [or rooms]: if it were not so, I would have told you. I go to prepare a place for you. And if I go and prepare a place for you, I will come again, and receive you unto myself; that where I am, there ye may be also" (John 14:1–3). Don't be fearful about the journey ahead; don't worry about where you are going or how you are going to get there. If you believe in the First Person of the Trinity, God the Father, also believe in the Second Person of the Trinity, the One who came as the Light of the World, not only to die for people, but to light up the way to a certain destination. This One, Jesus Christ, the Lamb of God, provides the ticket, is Himself the Light, will guide the footsteps along the way, and is even now preparing a specific, definite mansion or room as a place for us who are on our way. He not only promises with the absolute, certain promise of God that He is preparing the place, but states that He Himself will one day return to take us there in resurrected bodies (the dead in Christ will rise first, and then the living ones will be changed in a moment, in a twinkling of an eye, when He returns).

EDITH SCHAEFFER

Return, dear Lord, to those who look
   With eager eyes that yearn
For Thee among the garden flowers;
After the dark and lonely hours,
   As morning light return.

Return to those who wander far,
   With lamps that dimly burn,
Along the troubled road of thought,
Where doubt and conflict come unsought,—
   With inward joy return.

Return to those on whom the yoke
   Of life is hard and stern;
Renew the hope within their breast,
Draw them to Thee and give them rest:
   O Friend of Man, return.

Return to this war-weary world,
   And help us all to learn
Thy secret of victorious life,
The love that triumphs over strife,—
   O Prince of Peace, return.

Jesus, we ask not now that day
   When all men shall discern
Thy coming with the angelic host;
Today, to all who need Thee most,
   In silent ways, return!

HENRY VAN DYKE

Blessing,
   and honour,
      and glory,
      and power,
be unto him that sitteth upon the throne, and unto the Lamb
for ever and ever.

Revelation 5:13

Crown Him with many crowns,
  The Lamb upon His throne!
Hark how the heavenly anthem drowns
  All music but its own!
Awake, my soul, and sing
  Of Him who died for thee,
And hail Him as thy matchless King
  Through all eternity.

MATTHEW BRIDGES

Far simpler than any subsequent confession of faith which men have arrived at, the creed "Jesus is Lord" is nevertheless profound in its meaning and world-shaking in its consequences. To apply it faithfully involves asserting the absolute sovereignty of Jesus over every department of one's own life first, and then over all the life of the world. It means the throne of the universe for Christ. It is still a daring claim, as it was at the first; but no one who has honestly faced the fact of Christ can have any doubt at all that that throne is His by right. It has been bought with a price—bought with the hunger in the desert when He would not make the stones into bread; bought with the tears He shed over the sins of men; bought with the sweat of Gethsemane which was like great drops of blood; bought with the bitter cross where they broke His body in death; bought with the deathless love which through all the years has refused resolutely to let a lost world go. The Captain of the hosts of humanity has Himself been in the ranks. He has experienced the hardship and peril of life's campaign from the common soldier's side of it. He has endured the discipline. If He rides at the head of the host to-day, it is because He once marched on foot. If one day He is to be King over all the sons of men, it is because at the first He was not ashamed to call us brethren. "Wherefore," says Paul finely, summing up in that word the whole story of Jesus' sufferings and sorrows, "wherefore God also hath highly exalted Him, and given Him a name which is above every name, that at the name of Jesus every knee should bow" (Philippians 2:9).

JAMES S. STEWART

At the name of Jesus
  Every knee shall bow,
Every tongue confess Him
  King of glory now;
'Tis the Father's pleasure
  We should call Him Lord,
Who from the beginning
  Was the mighty Word.

CAROLINE M. NOEL

He that which these things saith, Surely,
I come quickly. Amen. Even so, come,
LORD Jesus.

Revelation 22:20

Lord Jesus, today might be the day when You will return! Our finite hearts cannot begin to comprehend all the glory that will be ours when we shall see You face-to-face! We live for the day when every knee shall bow to You, our Lord, our King of kings!

—J. W. B.

Acknowledgments

ABINGDON PRESS: Excerpt from *Life Is Forever* by Glenn Alty Crafts. Copyright © 1963 by Abingdon Press; excerpt from *Prescription for Anxiety* by Leslie D. Weatherhead; excerpts from *The Life and Teaching of Jesus Christ* by James S. Stewart. Used by permission of Abingdon Press.

ARGUS COMMUNICATIONS: Excerpts on pages 27, 28, 105, 119, are from *He Touched Me* by John Powell, © 1974 by John Powell. Used with permission of Argus Communications, Niles, Illinois.

AUGSBURG PUBLISHING HOUSE: Excerpt reprinted from *Prayer* by O. Hallesby, © 1931, 1959, by permission of Augsburg Publishing House.

BIBLE VOICE, INC.: Used with permission. Excerpt, Pat Boone, *Get Your Life Together*. Bible Voice, Inc., Van Nuys, CA © 1975.

CHOSEN BOOKS: Excerpt from *Adventures in Prayer* by Catherine Marshall. © Copyright 1975, published by Chosen Books Publishing Co., Ltd.; excerpts from *The Prayers of Peter Marshall*, edited by Catherine Marshall, Copyright © 1949. Used by permission of the Chosen Books Publishing Co., Ltd.

CHRISTIAN HERALD: "Christmas Eve" by Faith Baldwin, Copyright 1949 by *Christian Herald* and used by permission; excerpt from *The Secret of Serenity* by Gordon Powell is used by permission of *Christian Herald* (USA rights).

WILLIAM COLLINS, SONS & CO. LTD. (Canadian rights): Excerpts from the following books by C. S. Lewis are reproduced by permission of William Collins, Sons & Co., Ltd., London and Glasgow: *Miracles, Mere Christianity*, and *The Problem of Pain*; excerpts from *Jesus* by Malcolm Muggeridge reproduced by permission of William Collins, Sons & Co. Ltd., London & Glasgow (Canadian and British rights).

DAVID C. COOK PUBLISHING CO.: Excerpts reprinted from *Good News Is for Sharing* by Leighton Ford © 1977, David C. Cook Publishing Co., Elgin, IL 60120. Used by permission.

COSLETT PUBLISHING COMPANY: Excerpt from *Leaves of Gold* by A. E. Gregory is used by permission of the publisher.

THOMAS Y. CROWELL: Excerpt from pp. 104, 125, 126 in *The Cross on the Mountain* by Sherwood Eliot Wirt is reprinted on pp. 56, 160, 161. Copyright © 1959 by Sherwood Wirt. By permission of Thomas Y. Crowell.

PETER DAVIES LTD.: Excerpts from "The Verdict of the Empty Tomb" and "Were You There?" are from *Mr. Jones, Meet the Master* (British Edition) by Peter Marshall and are used by permission of Catherine Marshall.

DOUBLEDAY & CO., INC.: Excerpt from *Peace With God* by Billy Graham. Copyright © 1953 by Billy Graham; excerpts from *The Greatest Story Ever Told* by Fulton Oursler. Copyright 1949 by Fulton Oursler; excerpt from *Start Loving* by Colleen Townsend Evans. Copyright © 1976 by Colleen Townsend Evans and Laura Hobe; excerpt from *Life of Christ* by Fulton J. Sheen. Copyright © 1958 by Fulton J. Sheen. Used by permission of Doubleday & Company, Inc.

WILLIAM B. EERDMANS PUBLISHING COMPANY: Excerpts from *Convictions to Live By*, L. Nelson Bell, Copyright © 1966, William B. Eerdmans Publishing Company. Used by permission.

EVANGELICAL PUBLISHERS: "But We See Jesus" and "He Giveth More Grace" by Annie Johnson Flint are used by permission. Evangelical Publishers, Toronto, Canada.

FARRAR, STRAUS & GIROUX, INC.: "Prayer" from *Solzhenitsyn: A Pictorial Record* by Alexander Solzhenitsyn. © Editions du Seuil, 1974. English translation © 1974 by Farrar, Straus & Giroux, Inc. Reprinted with the permission of Farrar, Straus & Giroux, Inc.

SAMUEL FRENCH, INC.: "A Centurion Speaks to Mary" is from *The Terrible Meek* by Charles Rann Kennedy. Reprinted by permission of Samuel French, Inc.

GOSPEL LIGHT PUBLICATIONS: Excerpt reprinted from *Love Unlimited* by Bishop Festo Kivengere (Regal book). © Copyright 1975, Gospel Light Publications, Glendale, CA 91209. Used by permission.

THE BILLY GRAHAM EVANGELISTIC ASSOCIATION: "How Much Do You Love?" by H. A. Ironside from *Decision* © 1961, The Billy Graham Association; "There Came to Him a Woman" by Millie Dienert from *Decision* © 1967, The Billy Graham Association; "Why I Believe in God" by Winkie Pratney, from *Decision* © 1970, The Billy Graham Association; "This Too I Shall Give" by Ruth Graham from *Decision* © 1965, The Billy Graham Association; excerpts from *Day-by-Day* with Billy Graham. © 1976 by The Billy Graham Association. Excerpt from *Our Christmas Story* by Elizabeth Sherrill with Ruth Bell Graham © 1959 by The Billy Graham Evangelistic Association. Used by permission.

HARPER & ROW, PUBLISHERS, INC.: Excerpt from pp. 32–34 in *The Day Christ Was Born* by Jim Bishop is reprinted on p. 80, 81. Copyright © 1959, 1960 by Jim Bishop; excerpt from pp. 144–145 in *To Me It's Wonderful* by Ethel Waters is reprinted on p. 31. Copyright © 1972 by Ethel Waters; excerpts from pp. 79, 191 in *Jesus* by Malcolm Muggeridge are reprinted on pp. 106, 169. Copyright © 1975, by Malcolm Muggeridge (USA rights). Used by permission of Harper & Row Publishers, Inc.

189

HODDER & STOUGHTON LIMITED: "Indifference" and "Gambler" by G. A. Studdert-Kennedy are from *The Unutterable Beauty* and are used by permission of the publishers, Hodder & Stoughton Limited; excerpt from *The Secret of Serenity* by Gordon Powell is used by permission of Hodder & Stoughton Limited (British Commonwealth rights); excerpt from *The Greatest Drama Ever Staged* by Dorothy Sayers, published by Hodder & Stoughton Limited is used by permission of A. Watkins, Inc.

INTER-VARSITY PRESS: Excerpts are reprinted by permission from *Basic Christianity* by John R. W. Stott (© Inter-Varsity Press, Leicester; Eerdmans, Grand Rapids).

MACMILLAN PUBLISHING CO., INC.: Excerpts from the following books by C. S. Lewis are used by permission: *Miracles* (Copyright 1947 by Macmillan Publishing Co., Inc., renewed 1975 by Arthur Owen Barfield and Alfred Cecil Harwood): *Mere Christianity* (Copyright 1943, 1945, 1952 by Macmillan Publishing Co., Inc.), and *The Problem of Pain* (published in the United States by Macmillan Publishing Co., Inc., 1943); excerpt by Stopford Brooke is from *Handbook of Preaching Resources From English Literature*, compiled and edited by James Douglas Robertson (© James Douglas Robertson, 1962). Used by permission of Macmillan Publishing Co., Inc.

MANCHESTER UNIVERSITY PRESS: "Evil Days" by Boris Pasternak is used by permission of Manchester University Press.

MOODY PRESS: "Remembered Sin" and "Her Best for the Master" by Martha Snell Nicholson, Copyright, Moody Press, Moody Bible Institute of Chicago; excerpt from *Interludes in a Woman's Day* by Winola Wells Wirt, Copyright 1964. Moody Press, Moody Bible Institute of Chicago. Used by permission.

MULTNOMAH PRESS: *Parables by the Sea*, by Pamela Reeve, © 1976, Multnomah Press, Portland, Oregon. Used by permission.

JOHN OXENHAM'S poems are used by permission of Miss T. Oxenham.

PAULIST PRESS: Excerpt by Mother Teresa is from *To Give the Love of Christ* by James McGovern.

FLEMING H. REVELL COMPANY: Excerpts from *The Touch of the Master's Hand*. Copyright © 1956 by Fleming H. Revell Company; excerpt from *For Such a Time as This* by Vonette A. Bright, Copyright © 1976 by Fleming H. Revell Company; excerpts from *Some Run With Feet of Clay* by Jeannette Clift. Copyright © 1978 by Jeannette Clift George; excerpts from *A New Joy* by Colleen Townsend Evans. Copyright © 1973 by Fleming H. Revell Company; excerpts from *Creative Love* by Louis H. Evans, Jr. Copyright © 1977 by Louis H. Evans, Jr.; excerpts from *Because He Lives* by Gloria Gaither.

Copyright © 1977 by Gloria Gaither; excerpt from *Two From Galilee* by Marjorie Holmes. Copyright © 1972 by Marjorie Holmes Mighell; excerpts from *Rabboni* by W. Phillip Keller. Copyright © 1977 by W. Phillip Keller; excerpts from *I Came to Love You Late* by Joyce Landorf. Copyright © 1977 by Joyce Landorf; excerpts from "The Problem of Falling Rocks" and "The Touch of Faith" by Peter Marshall are from *Mr. Jones, Meet the Master*. Copyright © 1949, 1950 by Fleming H. Revell Company; excerpt from *What Jesus Says* by Robert Boyd Munger. Copyright © 1955 by Fleming H. Revell Company; excerpts from *God's Promises for You*. Copyright © 1977 by Roger C. Palms; excerpt from *My Prayer for You* by Pat Robertson. Copyright © 1977 by M. G. Robertson; excerpts from *Where He Leads* by Dale Evans Rogers. Copyright © 1974 by Fleming H. Revell Company; excerpts from *A Way of Seeing* by Edith Schaeffer are Copyright © 1977 by Edith Schaeffer; excerpt from *The Trouble With Alcohol* by Tom Shipp. Copyright © 1978 by Eloise DeLois Shipp; excerpt from *In My Father's House*. Copyright © 1976 by Corrie ten Boom and Carole C. Carlson; excerpt from *Each New Day*. Copyright © 1977 by Corrie ten Boom; excerpt from *He Cares, He Comforts* ("Jesus Is Victor" series) by Corrie ten Boom. Copyright © 1977 by Corrie ten Boom. Used by permission.

SPCK: "Lord, Thou Has Suffered" by Amy Carmichael is from *Rose From Brier;* "Have We Not Seen" by Amy Carmichael is from *Toward Jerusalem;* used by permission of SPCK.

TYNDALE HOUSE PUBLISHERS: Excerpts from *It's Incredible* by Ann Kiemel, published by Tyndale House Publishers, © Copyright 1977; excerpts from *The Cup of Wonder* by Lloyd John Ogilvie, published by Tyndale House Publishers, © Copyright 1976; excerpt from *He Is There and He Is Not Silent* by Francis Schaeffer, published by Tyndale House Publishers, © Copyright 1972; excerpts from *His Name Is Wonderful* by Warren Wiersbe, © Copyright 1976. Used by permission of Tyndale House Publishers.

WORD BOOKS: Excerpts from *How to Be Born Again* by Billy Graham, Copyright © 1977; excerpts from *Sitting by My Laughing Fire* by Ruth Bell Graham, Copyright © 1977; excerpts from *Life Without Limits* by Lloyd John Ogilvie, © Copyright 1975. Used by permission of Word Books, Publishers, Waco, Texas.

ZONDERVAN CORPORATION: Excerpt from *A Shepherd Looks at Psalm 23* by W. Phillip Keller is used by permission of the Zondervan Corporation; excerpts from *Illustrations for Preachers and Speakers* by Keith L. Brooks. Copyright 1946 by Zondervan Publishing House; excerpts from *Joni* by Joni Eareckson and Joe Musser, Copyright © 1976 by Joni Eareckson and Joe Musser. Used by permission of Zondervan Corporation.

Author Index